Bereshit
The Book
of the Beginning

Bereshit
The Book
of the Beginning

*A New Translation with
Commentary*

DAVID B. FRIEDMAN

WIPF *&* STOCK · Eugene, Oregon

BERESHIT, THE BOOK OF THE BEGINNING
A New Translation with Commentary

Scriptures taken from the Holy Bible, New International Version®, NIV®.
Copyright © 1973, 1978, 1984 by Biblica, Inc.™
Used by permission of Zondervan. All rights reserved worldwide

Talmud tractates Berakhot, Eruvim and Ta'anit
The Soncino Press, ltd.
123 Ditmas Avenue
Brooklyn, NY 11218

Verses taken from the Talmud, Tractates Pesachim, Rosh Hashanah, Shabbat and Ta'anit, Soncino Edition (R).
Copyright (c) 1998 by The Jewish Virtual Library.
Used by permission of the American-Israeli Enterprise.

Wipf & Stock
An Imprint of Wipf and Stock Publishers
199 W. 8th Ave., Suite 3
Eugene, OR 97401

www.wipfandstock.com

ISBN 13: 978-1-60608-734-3

Manufactured in the U.S.A.

In honor of my parents,
Nissim and Danna Friedman,
of blessed memory,
and Rabbi David Aronson,
peace be upon him.

In memory of my friends who have perished before their time:
Eitan, Ilan and Yoel.

Contents

Foreword

*B*ERESHIT, *THE BOOK OF the Beginning*, an ambitious undertaking to say the least, is a wonderful volume. Dr. David Friedman takes the reader through this amazing first book of the Torah, and of the Bible itself. Truly as the Hebrew title *Bereshit* ("in the beginning") indicates, it is a book of numerous profound beginnings. The amazing narrative begins before the very mists of time itself, when God spoke—perhaps "sang," as C. S. Lewis suggests—the universe into existence. In the miniscule fragments of micro seconds, the multiple dimensions of our vast universe were compressed into the dimensions of space and time with which we are familiar. In the opening chapters of Bereshit, we discover the formation of our planet and the creation of God's complex human creatures, as well as his shaping of the animal and plant worlds. We learn of the first revolt—that of the humans against their God—the first sacrifice, the first murder, and the first flood. These colossal events, and more, rush the reader in the span of eleven brief chapters. It's as if the narrator is speeding through the important preliminaries to arrive at his main theme. Eleven chapters cover thousands of years; the final thirty-nine chapters of Bereshit deal with little more than a century, but what a century! It appears that God is focusing our attention on the events of that century or so.

The renowned medieval rabbi and scholar Rashi raised an important question. Why does the Torah, he asked, begin with the account of creation—and we might extrapolate—and Bereshit? Why when it might more easily have begun with the Exodus and God's first commandment to his select nation: "This shall be the beginning of months for you," (Ex. 12.2) referring to the celebration of the momentous events of the Passover story? Another classic medieval rabbi and scholar, Nachmanides (Ramban), grappled with this question over a century later. He concluded that it was clear that God's creation—and its unfolding ramifications through the rest of Bereshit—stands at the center of Jewish religious thought. Bereshit remains the core and foundation for all that transpires later throughout world history as God guides our world toward its intended climax.

Those crucial thirty-nine chapters trace the story of Abraham and Sarah, Isaac and Rebekah, Jacob and Leah and Rachel, and the thirteen—Jacob had at least one daughter! This part of our amazing narrative details God's promises and dealings with those whom he selects as his "special people." These accounts stress that God "promises and performs"; he enters into a covenant (contract) with our ancestors and delivers on his commitments, time after time. Through it all, the narrative reminds us that God's covenant commitments are irrevocable, tangible and unconditional (gracious to the core). That covenant becomes foundational for the rest of the story that Moses unfolds for us through the Torah, and it shapes the unwrapping of God's purposes for his world—and through our history—as recorded in the rest of the Scriptures.

Unfortunately, the story of one of the key actors is frequently misconstrued and his character maligned. Rabbi Friedman does much to correct this misreading of Jacob. Jacob, after all, is a name (and man) of great blessing. His name testifies to the God who acts as his (Jacob's) defending rear guard; it uses terminology similar to that found in the verse (Isa. 52.12) preceding the amazing revelation of God's ultimate atoning sacrifice—and action "defending" us—described in Isaiah 52.13—53.12! As Rabbi Friedman rightly observes regarding Genesis 28: "Rivka and Yakov understood Esav's makeup and his disdain for God's purposes, and so they acted aggressively to insure that the covenants would not be inherited by Esav." This is but one example of Rabbi Friedman's astute perceptiveness and insight, as well as his thorough knowledge and scholarship. These same skills also served him well in his earlier works such as *They Loved the Torah* and *Who Knows Rabbi Arika?*

Some more morsels from this tasty treat follow. Commenting further on Genesis 28, Dr. Friedman notes concerning Jacob's assumed conditional vow or deal with God:

> However, Yakov had already been assured that God would be with him. I see this verse as a vow made out of gratefulness in reaction to God's promises of protecting Yakov and providing marvelously for his descendents (cf. v. 15). So, "God will be known as my God" (v. 21) because everyone would know that He brought Yakov back and provided for him, just as He promised. His faithfulness would be known to all. I do not view this as an "if you scratch my back, I'll

scratch yours" deal, as if one could do such a thing with Almighty God! Instead, it is a faithful response to the great promises of the Holy One of Israel.

One final illustration of the treasures found in this volume suggests the words of another rabbi (Rom. 6—7) and reflects those of an ancient prophet (Ezek. 36.25–27).

> The Ramban notes that when the Messiah comes, men will choose to do good instead of evil. He writes that the desire to do evil is the outcome of Adam and Eve's eating of the forbidden fruit: "But during the days of the Messiah, the selection between good and evil will be instinctive for them (mankind). Their hearts will not crave that which is not fit. They will not desire it at all."

In this delightful volume Dr. Friedman uses easy, idiomatic English while remaining true to the intent of the Hebrew text. Throughout, he makes excellent use of rabbinic sources both to unwrap and to illustrate strategic verses of the sacred text. Dr. Friedman has admirably accomplished his purpose of giving his readers an accessible and enlightening introduction to a foundational book of our Scriptures.

Rabbi Dr. John Fischer
Rosh Yeshiva, Netzer David International Yeshiva
President for Academic Affairs
St. Petersburg Theological Seminary, FL

Introduction

I HAVE ENDEAVORED TO render this version true to the meaning of the Masoretic text while making an idiomatic and easily understandable translation into English. I attempted to take into account each and every word from the Masoretic text, however, not as a word-for-word translation. Instead, I focused upon a phrase-by-phrase, sentence-by-sentence understanding. Sometimes I chose to make a conceptual rendition as opposed to a stiff English translation of what is very idiomatic Hebrew. At times there is a very thin line between translation and interpretation. I have tried to explain some linguistic aspects of Bereshit in my notes. However, at times I found it necessary to interpret given verses through my translation (as all translations, in the end, do).

Centuries ago, the Jewish sage Rabbi Yishma'el emphasized that although the Torah (Bible) is written in human language, it transmits a Heavenly message. He spent his career in the second century teaching particular methods of understanding the Torah through his finely developed thirteen methods of interpretation. Today, as in Rabbi Yishma'el's time period, translating and interpreting the Torah remains an immense challenge. Today's Jewish and Christian world, and our translators of the scriptures, still deal with human languages and finite understanding while simultaneously transmitting Heavenly narratives, principles, and instruction. I certainly appreciate Rabbi Yishma'el's grasp of the complexity of understanding the words of the Torah.

Throughout this translation, I put Hebrew names into English forms that preserve a likeness to the Hebrew name. Thus, I write "Avram" instead of "Abram," "Yakov" instead of "Jacob." The glossary at the end of this translation will list these relevant names. I did not use a Hebraicized form for the name "Isaac," as it is difficult to pronounce for English speakers. I ignore it in lieu of the English name. I also kept "Joseph" intact, due to the popularity of this biblical figure in western culture, instead of using his Hebrew name. Most names found in the text's chronologies have been given a phonetically based translation, so that the original Hebrew name is best preserved. As a result, some names may look strange to the reader, yet they do best reflect the original name as preserved in the Masoretic text.

In the end, individuals may translate the holy Torah, but it is up to our communities to relay its true meaning by the way in which we live out its messages.

Dr. David Friedman
Tishrei 5770 (September 2009)
Phoenix, AZ

Blessed are You, Lord our God, King of the Universe, Who has sanctified us by His commandments and commanded us to be busy studying the Torah.

> ". . . the Torah (Bible) is fire, was given from the midst of fire, and may be compared to fire. What is the nature of fire? If a man comes too close to it, he gets burned. If he keeps too far from it, he gets cold. The only thing for him to do is to seek to warm himself before its flames."
>
> —from the Mekilta of Rabbi Yishma'el (a midrashic work on the book of Exodus).

Chapter 1

1   At the very beginning, God dynamically created the heavenly bodies and the earth.[1]

2   Earth was chaotic and without order, and darkness blanketed earth's surface. God's spirit hovered over the waters.

3   Then God declared, "Let light exist!", and light came into being.

4   Since God knew that the light was good, He separated the light from the darkness.[2]

5   God named the light "day," and the darkness "night."

6   Together, evening and morning made up the entire first day.[3]

1.   *v.* 1: By dynamically, I mean with incredible power and action. The Torah gives us a picture of a moving, explosive speaking of God's energy that burst into creative action. When one realizes that there are some 100 billion galaxies that we know of, perhaps we gain some sense of the power that the Almighty is depicted as using in creating the heavenly bodies.

2.   *v.* 4: This phrase, "God knew that it was good" (Hebrew: *va'yar Elohim ki tov*, literally reads, "God saw that it was good." In ancient Jewish thought, *seeing* something's true reality and perceiving its real meaning meant to "know it." That is the sense that the text is giving to us in both v. 4 and in verses 10, 12 and 17. In v. 21 this same phrase is used, and its sense is amplified in that God declared His entire creation *very* good. God's declaration that light should exist was quite dynamic, i.e., "(God) speaks" (verse 1.3). "The result is light, the energizing of the vast cosmos through the marvelous electro-magnetic force system which maintains all structures and processes in matter. These varied energies include not only visible light, but also all the short-wave radiations (ultraviolet, x-rays, etc.) and the long-wave radiations (infrared, radio waves, etc.), as well as heat, sound, electricity, magnetism, molecular interactions, etc. 'Light,' the most basic form of energy, is mentioned specifically, but its existence necessarily implies the activation of all forms of electro-magnetic energies" (taken from http://www.icr.org/bible/gen/). From this short description of what 1.3 entailed, we get a picture for how detailed, intricate, and powerful the reality is that was spoken into being. I refer the reader to two excellent works that explore the relationship between the biblical text of creation and modern science: one is *Permission to Believe*, by Lawrence Kelemen, the other is *Genesis and the Big Bang Theory*, by Gerald Schroeder. An excellent on-line article addresses the creation of the world from both a traditional Jewish and scientific point of view. It is from Dr. Moshe Kaveh, and is found at http://www.biu.ac.il/JH/Parasha/eng/bereshit/kaveh.Html.

3.   *v.* 6: When the Torah states that "evening and morning were . . . ," perhaps a more pictorial image is being given to us. Instead of literally understanding the text as referring

7   Then God said, "There will be a separating space in the midst of the waters, and it will divide between the waters that are above the space from those that are below the space." Then it happened that way.

8   So God made the separating space, and it divided between the waters. God named this space the "sky." Together, evening and morning made up the entire second day.

9   God then said that the waters under the sky shall gather in one place, giving way to dry land. And it happened that way.

10 So God named the dry land "the ground," and the pooling of waters He named "the seas";

God knew that this was good.

11 Then God said, "The ground will sprout grasses and plants on the earth, and will produce fruit trees that bear fruit of its given species, with reproductive seeds within it." And it happened that way.

12 So the ground bore grasses and plants, each producing reproductive seeds of its own species, as well as fruit trees that each reproduced after its own kind. And God knew that this was good.

13 Together, evening and morning made up the entire third day.

14 Then God said, "There will be lights in the sky of the heavens to separate between day and night, and to be signs of the appointed times, to mark the days and the years.[4]

15 They will function as lights in the sky of the heavens, providing light for the earth." And it happened that way.

---

to the entities of "evening and morning," perhaps the text is telling us that the "time of darkness" combined with the "time of light" when combined together comprised the total day. This makes scientific sense if we think of a 24-hour long day. The Hebrew can be rendered either way—as specifically referring to actual dusk and early sunrise hours only, or to more general daily times of darkness and light.

4. v.14: "Appointed times" is the Hebrew word mo'adim. Here it specifically refers to marking off days and years; in Leviticus 23, mo'adim takes on more specified times and meanings. Leviticus 23 does not give another meaning to this same word, but further expands and clarifies 1.14. One of the brilliant aspects of the Torah is how it often later clarifies an earlier presented phrase or concept.

16 God made two great lights, the greater light (the sun) to rule over the day, and the lesser light (the moon) to rule over the night. God also fashioned the stars.

17 Then God set them in the sky of the heavens to provide light for the earth,

18 and to rule over day and night, as well as to separate between light and darkness. God knew that this was good.

19 So, together, evening and morning made up the entire fourth day.

20 Then God said, "The seas will be filled with aquatic life; and birds will fly over the earth, in the firmament of the sky."

21 So God created dinosaurs, each species after its own kind. And God knew that this was good.[5]

22 Then God blessed them, saying, "Multiply in number, and fill the seas; but the birds will multiply on dry land."

23 So, together evening and morning made up the entire fifth day.

24 Then God said, "The dry land will be the habitat for animals, each one reproducing after its own species—domestic animals, reptiles and wild animals, each fitting their own species." And it happened that way.

25 So God formed animal life on dry land, each according to its species; both domestic animals according to their species and reptiles according to their species. God knew that this was good.

26 Then God said, "Let's create humans in our image, according to our features; they will have dominion over the fish of the sea, the birds of the sky, domestic animals, and over all earth, including the reptiles that crawl on land."[6]

5. *v.* 21: Perhaps dinosaurs are meant by the phrase "big amphibians." This is just a thought, and is not a popular tradition that I am aware of. The Hebrew text could also be rendered "many sea creatures," and simply refer to aquatic life. Thus, "dinosaurs" is my translation and interpretation of the intent of the Hebrew words, but this remains conjecture. In such a reading, these "big amphibians" could have been totally destroyed in the flood of chapters 7–9 of our text.

6. *v.* 26: By "according to our features," I believe that the text refers to metaphysical (spiritual, emotional and mental) characteristics, and not to physical features. To quote Rabbi Yosef Soloveitchik (d. 1993), "according to our features" means: "There is no doubt that the term 'image of God' . . . refers to man's inner charismatic endowment as a cre-

27 So God created mankind in His image. He created mankind in God's image; He made them male and female.

28 Then God blessed them, saying to them, "Reproduce and be numerous, fill the earth and take it over; take dominion over the fish of the sea, the birds of the air and over all reptiles that crawl on the ground."

29 God then said, "Look, I am providing you with all kinds of vegetation and seeds that are found over the entire earth; every fruit tree that is found will provide you with food.[7]

30 Every animal on earth, bird of the sky, and reptile on land, every living creature, will eat from all kinds of green vegetation." And it happened that way.

31 God took stock of everything that He made, and indeed, it was very good! Together, evening and morning made up the entire sixth day.

---

ative being" (*The Lonely Man,* 12). I refer the reader to his work *The Lonely Man of Faith* for his fuller treatment of the meaning of man being created "according to our features." *v.* 26 uses the *pluralis majestatis,* the "royal we," in reference to God; cf. Bereshit 11.7. As the reader is aware, this plural form is used to describe one or more of the following possibilities: that God speaks in the plural because he addresses His heavenly beings (the angels); thus He is the King holding His royal court; or because He, as King of the Universe, is using what is considered a "kingly mode" of address. There is also the opinion extant that the Messiah pre-existed creation, and thus is among the Heavenly beings addressed in these verses (cf. Pesahim 54a, Nedarim 39a, Bereshit Rabbah 1.4, 2.4, 1 Enoch 62.7–9; references taken from *The Messiah Texts* by Raphael Patai). The implications of being created in God's image, in Jewish thought, are incredibly important. This fact gives mankind a special purpose. As Schonfeld wrote: "By divine design, Adam has speech—and all this entails about the human intellect. If he truly desires . . . he can reach the understanding of the cause of causes in all things, and come to bear witness to divine providence affecting the world" (*To Fathom Darkness,* 75). Thus Rabbi Schonfeld sees the first man as a prototype of all of humanity—gifted by God with the capacity to see God's providential ways, and therefore able to testify to His reality. The Jewish world in history has encouraged mankind to study the natural sciences, Biblical literature, psychology and many other fields of endeavor—all with the purpose of bearing witness to God's creative works. Schofeld makes reference to this overall view.

7. *v.* 29: It appears that the first man was created to be a vegetarian. Rabbinic sources in tractate Sanhedrin in the Talmud make note of this in saying: "R. Jehudah said in the name of Rabh: Adam the First was not permitted to eat meat. As it reads (Genesis 1.29–30): "To you it shall be for food, and to every beast of the field," meaning, but not the beasts to you. However, after the descendants of Noah came, he permitted them. As it reads (Genesis 9.3): "Every moving thing that liveth shall be yours for food: even as the green herbs have I given you all things." (http://www.jewishvirtuallibrary.org/jsource/Talmud/sanhedrin7.html).

Chapter 2

1 So the heavens and the earth, with all their varied parts, were finished.

2 God completed His creative work that He had done by the seventh day. Therefore, He rested on the seventh day from carrying out any more of His creative work such as He had done.

3 Then God blessed the seventh day and separated it (from the other days). He rested on it from His creative work through which He had formed His creation.

4 This is the history of the creation of the heavens and the earth at the time that the Lord God made earth and the heavens.[1]

5 This is before underbrush of the field existed and before grasses grew, since God had not yet made rain fall on the ground and mankind had not yet farmed the soil.

6 Mist used to rise from the ground and it watered the entire surface of the earth.

7 So, the Lord God formed man from the dust of the ground and infused through his nose the very breath of life. Then man became a living being.[2]

8 And from the very beginning, the Lord God planted a garden in Eden, a place of delight, and He put the man there whom He created.[3]

1. *v.* 4: The mention of the "heavens and the earth" is made twice in this verse. The first time the Hebrew reads "heavens and the earth," and the second time it reads "earth and the heavens." Perhaps this word order in the first instance is meant to be more chronological (time- and history-oriented; i.e., the heavens were created *before* the earth, and thus are mentioned first for that reason). Or perhaps because the sheer size of the heavenly bodies so dwarfs the earth that therefore due to the heavens' greater magnitude, they are mentioned first. The second use is more anthropocentric; i.e., mankind (who *live on earth*) is the crown of God's creation, and so the earth is put first in the word order to subtly emphasize this nuance.

2. *v.* 7: This is a very poetic way in Hebrew to simply say that God caused man to breathe air, after which man had life.

3. *v.* 8: There are some nuances about the Hebrew word *qedem*, which I translate as "from the very beginning." In one understanding, *qedem* refers to the period before

9   God caused pleasant-looking trees that bore tasty fruit to grow out of the ground. (He also put) the tree of life in the midst of the garden, as well as the tree by which to know good and evil.

10   In addition, a river that watered the garden flowed from Eden. From there it split into four tributaries.

11   One of the tributaries was the Pishon, and it ran through the land of Havilah, where gold was located.

12   The gold of that region was good, and crystal was found there along with onyx.

13   The name of the second tributary was the Gihon, and it ran through the entire land of Cush.

14   And the name of the third tributary was the Hiddekel. It went through eastern Assyria; finally, the fourth tributary was the Perat.

15   Then the Lord God took the man and placed him in the garden of delight, to work in it and to tend it.[4]

16   So the Lord God spoke a command to the man, saying "You can eat from every tree in the garden,

17   but don't eat from the tree of knowing good and evil, because on the day that you eat from it, you will definitely die."

18   Then the Lord God said, "It's not good for the man to be alone. I will make for him a helper to complement him."

19   The Lord God had formed all the wild animals and all the birds of the sky from the ground. He brought them to the man to see what he would name each one. Whatever the man called the living creatures became their name.[5]

---

the creation of time as we know it. Thus, an alternative rendering can be "from before the very beginning (of creation)." This idiomatic usage would be informing us that the garden was planned by God before the creation of earth itself.

4. *v.* 15: The word used in Hebrew for "work" is the same one as is used for "manual labor" and is also used for "worshipping God." The picture we get of the man's work is that it was not backbreaking labor by which he hoped to eke out a living. That *does* happen later in the text. At this point, his "work" consists of "tending" the garden and delighting in God's creation, which perhaps better fits a definition of "worship."

5. *v.* 19: The man takes part in God's creative activity, partnering with God and helping to complete His creation in some sense. This gives us insight into the meaning of 1.26,

20 So man named all the animals and birds; that is, all the creatures of the field. But there was no helper who could complement him.

21 Therefore, the Lord God put the man into a coma, and he slept. Then He took one of his ribs and closed up the skin over it.

22 And the Lord God built the rib that He took from the man into a woman, and He brought her to him.

23 So the man said, "This time, I see something like myself, flesh from my flesh," and he called her "woman," since she was taken from man.[6]

24 Because of this, a man will leave his father and mother's household and unite with his wife; they will unite in oneness.[7]

25 Both the man and his wife were naked and felt no shame about it.

---

where the man is formed in "the image" of God. Part of God's "image" is to be a creative being, as He is; and this is what the man does in this verse—creative activity, like that which God did.

6. *v.* 23: In this verse, the man first compares his new complement to the former creatures that he had seen: "this time" there was a "match" to complement him. In Hebrew, the word for "woman" is a derivative of the word for "man," with "*ish*" meaning "man," and "*ishah*" meaning "woman." Thus, we have a bit of a pun, but one that linguistically attests to the close relationship between man and woman. I believe the language is telling us that the man saw something that closely resembled himself (the Hebrew word "*etsem*," or "bone" may be an idiom, as it is in modern Hebrew, for "one's self"). Just as God had created the man in His image, so had He created a woman who closely resembled man, and the first man recognized this fact immediately. To some extent, it was as if the man looked at himself in a mirror and was amazed at what he saw. The Torah text preserves the man's reaction to seeing the woman.

7. *v.* 24: It is a remarkable finding of modern science that the story of one original male and one original female progenitor is factual. As the recent *Mystery of Science* magazine stated: ". . . using computer DNA sequencing technology, scientists are beginning to solve some of the mysteries of our genetic past. Their findings . . . corroborate the biblical claim that everyone on Earth has a common female and male ancestor—an original 'Adam' and 'Eve'. . ." (Bernstein, "Endless Enigmas," 6). As well, in a discussion of the human Y chromosome, Wade noted: "Every Y chromosome that exists today is a copy of the same original, carried by a single individual in the ancestral human population" (Wade, "Adam, Eve and the Genome," 46). Again he writes: "The same is true of mitochrondrial DNA. The metaphor is hard to avoid—this is Adam's Y chromosome, and Eve's mitochrondrial DNA; everyone, male and female, carries the same mitochrondrial DNA because all are copies of the same original, the mitochondrial DNA belonging to a single woman" (ibid., 46).

Chapter 3

1   But the snake was more devious than any other animal of the field that the Lord God had created. It said to the woman, "Now did God really say, 'Don't eat from any of the trees of the garden?'"[1]

2   The woman answered the snake, "We can eat from the fruit of the trees of the garden.

3   But from the fruit of the tree that is in the middle of the garden, God said, 'Don't eat from it, and don't touch it, or you will die.'"

4   Then the snake said to the woman, "Come on! You won't die!

5   Actually, God knows that on the day that the two of you eat from it, your eyes will open up and you will be just like God, knowing both good and evil!"

6   Then the woman saw that the fruit tree looked delicious and was sensual to the eyes. Because the tree was desirable for becoming knowledgeable, she took from its fruit and ate it. Then she gave some to her husband who was with her, which he ate.[2]

7   As a result, their eyes were opened, and they knew that they were naked. So, they sewed fig leaves together and made coverings.[3]

8   Following this, God's voice was heard going through the garden during the windy time of the day. The man and his wife hid from the Lord God in the midst of the trees of the garden.

1.   *vv.* 1–4: When God told the man and woman that they would die, it is clear that He didn't mean an immediate death. The Targum Yonatan translates 2.17 as: "For on the day in which you eat of it, you shall be guilty of death." As Rabbi Shlomo Riskin has noted: ". . .that is, judged worthy of death, but not necessarily suffer an immediate execution" (Riskin, "There is Still Time"). Physical death became the eventual fate of these first two humans, as well as the fate of their descendants.

2.   *v.* 6: Bereshit Rabbah identified this tree as a fig tree, based on the fact that the leaves that were sewn together by the man and woman were fig leaves. Other rabbi-commentators have made various conjectures as to the identity of the fruit, including grapes, wheat (!), and apples. See Rabbi Yose's comment in Bereshit Rabbah to Genesis 15:7.

3.   *v.* 7: "Coverings" describes the function of these leaves; the Hebrew word *hagorot* may refer to a belt or midsection undergarment, possibly a type of wrap.

9   So the Lord God called out to the man and said to him, "Where are you?"

10 (The man) answered, "I heard your voice in the garden, and I was afraid because I was naked, so I hid."

11 And (God) said, "Who told you that you were naked? Did you eat from the tree from which I instructed you never to eat?"

12 Then the man replied, "The woman that you gave me, she gave it to me off of the tree, and I ate it."

13 So the Lord God said to the woman, "What did you do?" The woman answered, "The snake misled me, and so I ate it."

14 The Lord God then spoke to the snake, "Because you did this, you are cursed above and beyond any other creature and animal of the field. You will crawl on your stomach, and you will eat dust for your entire life.

15 I have also decreed that hostility will exist between you and the woman, and between your descendants and hers; (her descendant) will crush your head, but you will nip at his heels."

16 He then said to the woman, "I will greatly increase your suffering in childbirth; in pain you will bear children, and you will desire your husband. He will have authority over you, to protect you."

17 He said to the man, "Because you took your wife's advice and you ate from the tree that I instructed you about, saying that you should not eat from it, the ground will be cursed because of you. During your entire lifetime, you will eat the ground's produce only through hard work.

18 Therefore, you will find thorns and thistles growing (from the ground), and you will eat the vegetation of the field.

19 By the sweat of your eyebrows you will eat bread till the day you die. Because you were made from dust, you will return to dust."

20 The man named his wife "Chava" because she was the mother of all human life.[4]

---

4. *v.* 20: The name Chava is connected to the word "life" (*chay*) in Hebrew.

21 Then the Lord God made animal skin clothing for the man and his wife, to dress them.

22 The Lord God said, "The man is like one of us, knowing good from evil. So in order that he doesn't try to take anything from the tree of life and eat it, then live forever . . ."[5]

23 the Lord God exiled him from the garden of delight, so that he would farm the very ground from which he was created.

24 And so He expelled the man. Then winged beings were stationed in front of the garden of delight, along with the rotating, flaming sword that guarded the way to the tree of life.[6]

5. v. 22: The Ramban notes that when the Messiah comes, men will choose to do good instead of evil. He writes that the desire to do evil is the outcome of Adam and Eve's eating of the forbidden fruit: "But during the days of the Messiah, the selection between good and evil will be instinctive for them (mankind). Their hearts will not crave that which is not fit. They will not desire it at all" (Singer, Ramban, 31).

6. v. 24: These "winged beings" are called cherubim in Hebrew. They are a type of angelic creature that are written about in Exodus 25.19 and 37.8, as well as some eleven times in the book of Ezekiel. Here their function is to serve as guards in the garden. The sword's motion is described in Hebrew as "mithapeket." This could refer to a circular type of movement ("revolving," as I translate it here), or to a dipping and "flipping over" motion. This word refers to a rotational movement. Whatever the motion itself entailed, it is clear that the sword's purpose was to restrict or prevent entry. Who would see the sword and be discouraged to enter the garden? This must be intended to keep the man and his wife (and possibly future descendants) from trying to return there.

Chapter 4

1   The man had sexual relations with Chava, his wife, and she became pregnant and gave birth to Cain. So she said, "I have gotten a child from the Lord."[1]

2   And again she gave birth, to his brother, Hevel, who became a shepherd. Cain was a farmer.[2]

3   After a passage of some time, Cain brought some ground produce as an offering to God.

4   Also Hevel brought of the first-born animals from his flock and from their fat produce. And God favored Hevel and his offering.

5   But God did not particularly favor Cain and his offering. So Cain was very angry, and he carried a sad facial expression.

6   So God told Cain, "Why are you so upset? Why do you look so down?

7   Don't you know that if you do what is right, you will live correctly before Me? But if you don't do what is right, you will miss the mark and desire to do what is wrong. So you must control your actions."[3]

8   Afterwards, Cain argued with his brother Hevel when they were together in a field. Cain became angry at Hevel, and so he murdered him.[4]

1. *v.* 1: The name Cain is connected to Chava's words in the Hebrew for "I have gotten" ("*qaniti*").

2. *v.* 2: The name "Lemek" in Hebrew connotes a fool.

3. *v.* 7: Verse seven uses very idiomatic Hebrew. The text uses a very interesting word, *se'et*, which I have translated as "live correctly before Me." My thought is that this word, often used specifically in wedding and betrothal language, expresses a unity with God's purposes. It also expresses an ability to do something that was later expressed by God to Avraham via the Hebrew word *lehithalek*. This means to live in such a way as is pleasing to God.

4. *v.* 8: I translated the Hebrew phrase *vayahargayhu* as "so he murdered him." Although another word existed for "murder" in ancient Hebrew (*ratsach*; cf. Exodus 20.13), the evidence of the scriptures is that God considered Cain's action not just a mere "killing," but an unrighteous, uncalled-for and evil action, thus justifying my translation (cf. 4.10–11). Professor Dov Landau has an interesting take on Cain's motivation for

9   God then asked Cain, "Where is Hevel your brother?" Then he (Cain) answered, "I don't know. Am I my brother's guardian?"[5]

10 Then God said, "What did you do? Your brother's blood cries out loudly to me from the ground!

11 Because the ground has absorbed your brother's blood that you shed, you have brought curses upon yourself!

12 When you farm the ground, it will not be fruitful and yield crops for you. Instead, you will now be a nomad and wanderer throughout the earth."

13 Then Cain complained to God, "This is too harsh of a punishment for me to bear!

14 Today you banished me from everyone's presence, as well as from Your presence. I will be a nomad and wanderer upon the earth, and everyone who sees me will try to kill me."

---

murdering Hevel. He writes the following in his article "But to Cain and his offering He paid no heed": ". . . The expression *gam hu*, 'for his part,' (lit. 'also he') in the verse 'and Abel, for his part (Gen. 4.4) clearly indicates that Abel brought his offering after Cain had brought his, and that he had seen what Cain had brought. ....Abel's offering could be interpreted as competitiveness, or even as inciting Cain. Now Abel succeeded in this competition....Cain, for his part, perceived the situation as follows: after his initiative in bringing an offering, Abel came and 'upped the ante' for drawing near to God. Henceforth it would no longer suffice to bring an offering to God; rather, one would have to embellish that offering… the new situation made Cain feel totally helpless and aroused his ire. Cain became frustrated, and frustration is one of the most dangerous things" (http://www.biu.ac.il/JH/Parasha/eng/bereshit/lan.html).

5. *v.* 9: Rabbi Schonfeld has another interpretation of Cain's words in verses 7–9. He sees it as the commensurate interplay of God's foreknowledge and mankind's freedom of choice: "If you do good," He (God) goes on, immediately impressing upon him the reality of his free volition, "there will be special privilege." For Cain will have chosen freely, despite God's knowledge, and hence merits reward. "And if you do not do good"—that, too, is in your (Cain's) hands." (Schonfeld, 71). That is, Rabbi Schonfeld sees all mankind in a similar situation to Cain—like Cain, mankind is able to acknowledge God's ownership and rulership over the world, and consequently to do His instructions. Conversely, as Cain decided, mankind can choose not to care for others (e.g. as Cain put it, "Am I my brother's guardian?") and to disregard God's instructions (in this specific instance, His words in verse 7). May I add that Cain did not see reality in a proper perspective. He lied to God ("I do not know" of verse 9, when he clearly did know what happened to his brother). Perhaps a lesson that Bereshit's author wanted us to realize was that when God's ways are disregarded, humanity sees reality wrongly, is prone to violence, and believes lies (just as Cain did).

15 God then said to him, "So anyone who tries to kill Cain will suffer curses seven-fold . . . and God will put on Cain a sign so that all who find him will know not to attack him."

16 So Cain had to leave God's presence, and he settled in the region of Nod, just east of Eden.

17 Afterward, Cain had intimate relations with his wife, and she became pregnant and gave birth to Hanoch. [Cain] then built a town and named it Hanoch, after his son.

18 Hanoch had a son named Erad, and Erad had a son named Mehuya'el. Metuya'el fathered Metusha'el, who fathered Lamek.

19 Lamek took two women to be his wives. One was named Adah, and the second was named Silah.

20 Adah gave birth to Yaval, who was the patriarch of those who live in tents and breed livestock.

21 His brother was Yuval, who was the patriarch of musicians who play stringed instruments and flutes.

22 Silah bore Tuval-Cain, who wrought brass and iron, as well as Tuval-Cain's sister, Na'amah.

23 Then Lemek said to his wives Adah and Silah, "Listen to me, to Lamek; pay attention to my words. I killed someone who hurt me, as well as a child who bruised me.[6]

6. *v.* 23: This verse could refer to Lemek killing one and the same person, that is, a young man who had struck him, or two separate people—a man and, in addition, a youngster. The most accurate translation depends upon the meaning of the word "*ve*" in the text. I have chosen to translate this verse to indicate that two persons were slain. Historic Jewish translation does interesting things to this text. In one version of the Targum (2E), the translated Aramaic reads: "I did not kill a man, for whose sake I should be killed, and also I did not wound a young boy, on account of which my clan should be destroyed" (4.23, Clem translation). Thus, Babylonian Jewish translation (and interpretation) relays that Lemek was claiming his innocence, instead of boasting about his violent actions. 4.24 would seem to favor the "boasting" translation, given that Lemek seemed to have expected possible blood vengeance to be taken by the clan of the slain. The meaning of the numbers in "seven-fold" and "seventy-fold" curses is obscure. It may mean seven times the number of an understood curse for an unrighteous killing, which in the mouth of Lemek seems meaningless and twisted. But that is my conjecture.

The medieval Jewish sage the "*Ramban*" (acronym for Moshe ben Nachman; see glossary) has a different explanation. He wrote: ". . . have I killed a man for my injury and a

24 If seven-fold curses come upon anyone taking vengeance on Cain, seventy-fold curses will fall upon anyone taking vengeance on Lemek!"

25 The (first) man once again had intimate relations with his wife, and she bore a son, calling his name Seth, because "God has gifted me with another offspring in place of Hevel, since Cain killed him."

26 Seth also fathered a son, and named him Enosh. It was then that humanity began to worship God.

---

child for my wound? [I surely have not!] If Kayin [who murdered] shall be avenged sevenfold, then Lemech [who only produced weapons but did not himself use them] shall be avenged seventy-sevenfold!" (4.23–24)." Rabbi Hattin adds: "Perhaps there is even a note of sarcasm to be added to Lemech's defensive words, for he seems cavalierly unconcerned with his wives' anxiety. "What are you two fretting about?" he seems to exclaim, "I have done nothing wrong! Am I then like Kayin who murdered his own brother in cold blood?" (M. Hattin, "The Legacy of Kayin," http://vbm-torah.org/archive/intparsha 66/01-66bereishit.htm).

Chapter 5

1 This is the historic recounting of the first man, from the day on which God created man in His image.

2 He made them male and female, and He blessed them. Then He named them "mankind" on the day that He created them.

3 So this man was 130 years old when he fathered a son named Seth, who was born in his likeness and possessed his features.

4 The first man lived eight hundred years after the birth of Seth, and he fathered other sons and daughters.

5 The first man's entire lifetime was 930 years; then he died.

6 Seth was 105 years old when he fathered Enosh.

7 Seth lived another 807 years after fathering Enosh, and he fathered other sons and daughters.

8 Seth's entire lifetime was 912 years; then he died.

9 Enosh was ninety years old when he fathered Kaynan.

10 Enosh lived another 815 years after fathering Kaynan, and he fathered other sons and daughters.

11 Enosh's entire lifetime was 905 years; then he died.

12 Kaynan was seventy years old when he fathered Mahalalel.

13 Kaynan lived another 840 years after fathering Mahalalel, and he fathered other sons and daughters.

14 Kaynan's entire lifetime was 910 years; then he died.

15 Mahalelel was sixty-five years old when he fathered Yared.

16 Mahalelel lived another 830 years after fathering Yared, and he fathered other sons and daughters.

17 Mahalelel's entire lifetime was 895 years; then he died.

18 Yared was 162 years old when he fathered Hanok.

19 Yared lived another eight hundred years after fathering Hanok, and he fathered other sons and daughters.

20 Yared's entire lifetime was 962 years; then he died.

21 Hanok was sixty-five years old when he fathered Metushelach.

22 Hanok lived in scrupulous obedience to God; he lived another three hundred years after he fathered Metushelach, and he had other sons and daughters.

23 Hanok's entire life on earth was 365 years.

24 Hanok lived so righteously in the fear of God, that he was taken away; God Himself took him.

25 Metushelach was 187 years old when he fathered Lamek.

26 Metushelach lived another 782 years after he fathered Lamek, and he fathered other sons and daughters.

27 Metushelach's entire lifetime was 969 years; then he died.

28 Lamek was 182 years old when he fathered a son.

29 And he called his name Noach, saying, "He'll comfort us from our hard lot and from our difficult labor by which God has cursed us."[1]

30 Lamek lived another 595 years after he fathered Noach, and he fathered other sons and daughters.

31 Lamek's entire lifetime was 777 years; then he died.

32 Noah was five hundred years old, and he fathered Shem, Ham and Yafet.

---

1. *v.* 29: The name *Noah* (Hebrew, "Noach") means "comfort." Thus Lamek's words spoke of the role that his son would have in ensuing history.

Chapter 6

1   This was when mankind began to populate the earth. In particular, many daughters were born to people in that period.[1]

2   The sons of God knew that these young women were beautiful. So they picked out whomever they desired and took (them as) wives from among them.

3   So God said, "I won't fight with mankind forever, since they are frail and but human. So they will live to be only 120 years old."

4   Fallen beings were present on earth in those days (as well as afterward) when they coupled with women. Their offspring were mighty warriors who had great reputations from early on in history.[2]

---

1. *vv.*1–2: See the very interesting analysis of the lessons of this narrative found at http://www.ericlevy.com/Writings/Writings_BneiElohim.htm. Levy summarizes the wrongdoings of the "sons of God" as: ". . . enabling their hedonistic desires. More specifically. . . [their] purpose is to dominate the daughters of man (and, de facto, man himself) for the sake of unbounded physical pleasure."

2. *vv.* 4–5: These mighty warriors, the offspring of the sons of God, are identified as evil beings in the book of Hanoch: "They taught them [women] sorcery and incantations, how to cut roots and plants. And they gave birth to mighty giants 3,000 cubits high. [The giants] ate all that men could make until men could not longer sustain them. Then the great ones turned against and ate the men. And they began to sin against birds and beasts and crawly things, and to drink human blood. And Azzazael taught the children of men to make shields and armor . . . and taught them to make up their eyes and dyes, and of precious stones. . . ." (taken from www.ericlevy.com/ Writings/Writings_BneiElohim .htm). Levy then summarizes the book of Hanoch's viewpoint on the offspring of the sons of God: "Bestiality, cannibalism, war, and seduction; these mirror the sins of the Generation of the Flood." The book of Hanoch can be accessed at http://reluctant-messenger .com/book_of_enoch.htm and at http://www.sacred-texts.com/bib/boe/.

It is fascinating to read the Epic of Gilgamesh (see glossary) and to note the similarities between the figure of Gilgamesh and the "fallen ones" of *v.* 4. It is this author's conclusion that this is a possible extra biblical epic drama of one, if not two, of these "fallen beings," or their descendants. I refer the reader to The Epic of Gilgamesh, Tablet I:29–91, in particular. The Epic of Gilgamesh can be found at http://www.ancienttexts .org/library/mesopotamian/gilgamesh/tab1.htm.

In contrast to these 'fallen beings' who polluted mankind, we have Noah, who represented the line of mankind that had not been influenced by the 'fallen beings' or their offspring. He has no genealogical connection to them. The text infers that these are the reasons that his family was chosen to survive the flood (see 6.8–9).

5   God knew that mankind was engaging in much evil activity. The entire scope of every desire and plan of mankind was wicked.

6   In addition, God regretted that He had created mankind upon earth, and He was saddened about their state of being.

7   So God said, "I will put an end to mankind which I created, since I regret that I created them all—from men to animals, and reptiles as well as the birds of the air."

8   But Noah was favored by God.

9   This is the family history of Noah: Noah was a scrupulously righteous man who feared God. So he stood out among those of his generation, because he lived righteously before God.

10 Noah fathered three sons: they were Shem, Ham, and Yafet.

11 The earth was corrupt in its relation to God and was full of wanton violence.

12 Everything was perverted, because all mankind lived corrupt lifestyles on earth.

13 Then God told Noah, "All humanity is about to end, because all of earth is full of wanton violence. Men have perverted the entire earth.

14 So make for yourself a boat of buoyant wood; make animal pens in the boat, and coat it inside and outside with pitch.[3]

15 Make the boat 300 *amah* in length, 50 *amah* in width, and 30 *amah* in height.[4]

16 Make a roof for the boat, and build the vessel upward to an *amah* short of the roof. Put a door on the side of the boat, and build three decks on the vessel.

17 This is because I will definitely bring a catastrophic flood upon the earth, to destroy all animal and human life. Everything on earth is to be eradicated.

3. *v.* 14: The identification and translation of *gofer* wood (Hebrew) is uncertain. It has been identified as various types of known woods: acacia and cypress are among them. However, whatever type of wood it was, it was certainly buoyant.

4. *v.*15: An *amah* is the Hebrew word for a measure of approximately twenty or twenty-one inches in length.

18 But I will fulfill My covenant with you, because you, your wife, your sons and their wives will board the boat.

19 As well, bring a pair (one male and one female) from all the animals, to the boat.

20 (Bring them) from the birds, each pair according to its species; and from the animals of the field, each pair according to its species; also from the reptiles, bring two of each species, so that they may continue to live.

21 Then take and store up food of every variety, so that you can consume it. This will be the food supply both for you (humans) and for them (the animal life)."

22 So Noah did everything that God commanded him; he did it all.

Chapter 7

1   Then God instructed Noah, "Take your entire family, including yourself, to the boat, because I have paid attention that you are a righteous man among your peers.

2   Take seven pairs of each ritually pure animal, one male and one female to each pair, and take one pair of each ritually impure animal, one male and one female.

3   Also take seven pairs of each type of bird, male and female, so that they may live on the earth and be able to replenish it.

4   This is because in seven more days, I will cause rain to fall on the earth for forty days and nights—I will wipe out all creatures that I have made that live on the earth!"

5   So Noah did everything that God commanded him.

6   Noah was six hundred years old when this deluge flooded all the earth.

7   Then Noah, his wife, his sons and their wives entered the boat with him just before the floodwaters came.

8   and 9   The ritually pure animals and the ritually impure animals, as well as birds and reptiles, came to Noah and to the boat. They came in pairs of males and females, just as God commanded to Noah.

10 Then the floods occurred for seven days upon earth.

11 When Noah was six hundred years old, on the seventeenth day of the second month, all the water sources on earth and in heaven opened up.

12 So rain fell on earth for forty days and forty nights.

13 Actually on this day (the seventeenth day of the second month), Noah, Shem, Ham and Yafet, along with their wives, came into the boat.

14 They entered along with all different species of animal life, including reptiles of each species that crawl on the ground, and all types of winged species that fly, every type of bird and winged creature.

15 They all came with Noah aboard the boat, pair by pair, from every type of life.

16 Male and female from every type of life came aboard, as God had commanded him; God Himself closed (the entrance) for him (Noah).

17 The flooding occurred on the earth for forty days and nights, and the floodwaters mounted up, and carried the boat and lifted it up high above the ground.

18 So the floodwaters welled up greatly on earth, and the boat floated on the surface of the waters.

19 The floodwaters continued to greatly rise on the earth's surface, so that all the high mountains were underwater.

20 The floodwaters reached a height of fifteen *amah* above the mountaintops, and covered them over.[1]

21 All known life was eradicated—reptiles that crawl, birds, wild animals, all species of insect life that swarm over the earth, and all of mankind.

22 Every type of living being was destroyed and perished.

23 All beings, including humans, animals, reptiles and birds that lived on earth, were wiped out. Only Noah and everything that was present with him survived.

24 The floodwaters were at their maximum height on the earth for 150 days.

---

1. *v.* 20: As previously noted, the Hebrew word *amah*, sometimes referred to as a "cubit," is a measurement of up to twenty-one inches in height. Using this measurement, according to the text here, the water rose up to three hundred inches (approximately twenty-five feet or 8.3 yards) above the mountaintops.

Chapter 8

1 However, God remembered Noah as well as all the life and the animals that were with him in the boat. So God sent a wind over the earth, and the floodwaters receded.

2 Earth's water sources dammed up, and the rain clouds in the sky dried up, as the period for rainfall from the sky drew to a close.

3 The floodwaters steadily receded from the ground and had ceased from rising after the 150 days.

4 The boat came ashore on the Ararat mountain range on the seventeenth day of the seventh month.

5 And so the floodwaters continued to recede until the first day of the tenth month. It was then that the tops of mountains appeared.

6 At the end of forty days, Noah opened the door of the boat that he had built.

7 He then let a crow free, but it returned after leaving, until the waters had receded more off of the earth's surface.[1]

8 Afterwards, he let a dove free, to see if the water had further receded off of the earth's surface.

9 But the dove didn't find any resting spot for itself, so it returned to him (Noah) in the boat, because much water was still covering the earth's surface. So Noah took the dove in his hand and brought it into the boat.

10 Another seven days passed, and again he sent the dove out of the boat.

11 The dove returned to him at evening, and it held a plucked olive leaf in its mouth. Then Noah knew that the floodwaters had truly receded from the earth's surface.

12 Yet another seven days went by, and he again sent the dove out, and this time it did not return.

---

1. *v. 7*: The word for "crow" (*orev* in Hebrew) can also mean a raven.

13 So on the first day of the first month when he was 601 years old, the floodwaters were abated from the earth's surface. Noah took off the ark's covering; he looked and saw the dry, bare ground.

14 On the seventeenth day of the second month, the land was thoroughly dry.

15 Then God spoke to Noah, saying,

16 "You, your wife, your sons and their wives are to leave the boat.

17 Bring out all the creatures that are with you. All the types should come out: all birds, all animals and all the reptiles that crawl on the ground. They should spread out over the dry land, and be fruitful and reproduce."

18 And so Noah, his wife, his sons, and their wives all left.

19 Along with them, all animals, all reptiles, all birds, all creatures that crawl on the ground, each by its species, left from the boat.

20 Then Noah built an altar to worship the Lord. He took sacrifices from all types of ritually pure animals and from all types of ritually pure birds, and he offered them as whole burnt offerings on the altar.

21 God was greatly pleased with the sacrifice. He then said to Himself, "I will not curse the earth again because of mankind, just because every desire they have from their youth is evil. I will never again strike all life which I have created.

22 As long as earth exists, sowing and reaping seasons, cold and hot seasons: summer and winter, and day and night will never cease from occurring."

Chapter 9

1   Then God blessed Noah and his sons, saying to them, "Reproduce by having children, and fill the earth.

2   Every animal on earth, every bird in the sky, and everything that crawls on the ground, as well as all the fish of the sea, will fear you. They will be frightened of you and be subject to you.[1]

3   Every animal that moves and is alive will be your food, like green vegetation. I have provided you with all of this.

4   But don't eat any meat that still has blood in it.[2]

5   I will hold every living being responsible for the life of another. I will hold every human being responsible for the life of another; I will demand an accounting for each life.

6   Since man was made in God's image, whoever kills a person will be killed by others.[3]

7   But you, reproduce, have children, and become numerous throughout the earth: rule over it."

8   Then God spoke to Noah and his sons, saying,

9   "I will definitely fulfill my covenant with you and your descendants,

10 and with all the creatures that were with you, and left the boat with you; with the birds, animals, and all life on earth.

---

1. *v.* 2: This description of human-animal relations causes me to believe that the "large amphibians" previously mentioned, if they can be identified as dinosaurs, no longer existed by this time.

2. *v.* 4: This verse may also be rendered, "But don't eat any animal that is still alive." The intent of this *mitzvah* (commandment) is to forbid eating a live animal, and additionally to insure that a slaughtered animal is not eaten raw (as blood would still be in the meat). Both of these interpretations or translations are true to the Hebrew text and are parts of our kosher dietary laws.

3. *v.* 6: This *mitzvah* means that whoever murders a fellow human will be liable to capital punishment. The Hebrew word *tselem* (image) has significant meaning in the Torah. We can see the great value of human life when we understand this word. 1.26 notes that man was made in God's *tselem*. See my note to 1.26.

11 I will make my covenant with you by never again destroying all life by floodwaters. There will never again be a flood that will totally devastate the entire earth."

12 Then God said, "This is the sign of my covenant that I am making between me and you, and all animal life that is with you. It will last till eternity, for all generations.

13 I have made my rainbow in the clouds, and it is the sign of My covenant between Me and all of the earth.

14 So when I cause cloudy skies over the earth and My rainbow is seen in the clouds,

15 I will then remember my covenant between Me and you and all types of life. Never again will floodwaters devastate all life.

16 When you see a rainbow in the clouds, remember the eternal covenant between God and all types of living beings that are on earth."

17 Then God said to Noah, "This (the rainbow) is the sign of the covenant that I am making between Me and all life that is on earth."

18 The sons of Noah who left the boat were Shem, Ham, and Yafet. Ham was the father of Canaan.

19 These were Noah's three sons, and they filled and spread out over all the earth.

20. Noah became a farmer, and he planted a vineyard.

21 He drank from its wine, became intoxicated, and undressed inside his tent.[4]

22 So Ham, the father of Canaan, saw his father inappropriately, and he told this to his two brothers who were outside.[5]

---

4. *v. 21:* The word that is translated "to undress" may also mean that Noah behaved drunkenly and was discovered in this state inside his tent. Thus his actions were "uncovered."

5. *v. 22:* Thus, either Ham saw Noah naked or behaving like a drunkard. We can ask why Noah may have chosen to get intoxicated. An interesting opinion is offered by Rabbi Steinhardt: "Noah is the first survivor (of the flood). When he came out of the ark he saw that every single person he knew except for his immediate family had been killed. He saw all the destruction and he despaired. He saw (that) every house and every tree and everything that was familiar to him were wiped out" (taken from http://

23 Then Shem and Yafet took and carried an outer garment, and walked backward (into the tent). They covered their naked father while looking away. They did not see their father undressed.

24 When Noah recovered from being drunk, he knew what his youngest son had done.

25 He then said, "Cursed is Canaan; he will be a slave of slaves to his brothers."

26 He further said, "Blessed be the Lord God of Shem. Canaan will be his slave.

27 May God make Yafet expand his influence, and may he live under the protection of Shem. Canaan will be his slave, too."[6]

28 After the great flood, Noah lived another 350 years.

29 Noah reached the age of 950 years, and then he died.

---

www.bnai-torah.org/clientuploads/sermons/Rabbi_Steinhardt_Parsha_Noah_5768_2 .pdf). Then Steinhardt expresses another opinion, that of a colleague: "Rabbi Daniel Gordis, offers . . . (his) explanation. . . . (Noah) got drunk because he couldn't handle the success. . . . He actually had saved the world and he was the focus of the universe.... He did great things. He was on an incredible high and when he came off the ark. He now had to involve himself in the mundane. . . . That was very, very difficult for him. Rabbi Gordis refers to it as the "Noah Syndrome" (taken from http://www.bnai-torah .org/clientuploads/sermons/Rabbi_Steinhardt_Parsha_Noah_5768_2.pdf).

As a biographical note, Rabbi Gordis was vice president at the University of Judaism in Los Angeles and the dean of the Ziegler School of Rabbinic Studies there before immigrating to Israel. He now serves as the Senior Vice President of the Shalem Center in Israel.

6. v. 27 makes a pun of Yafet's name, since the Hebrew word for "expand" is from the same root. Yafet is portrayed as one who "expands" his territory and influence, while Shem (Hebrew for "name" and "good reputation") retained his good reputation in this blessing by his father. The name Ham (Hebrew for "hot," maybe "hot-headed," if it refers to Ham's temperament), may denote his derogatory or degrading words to his brothers about their father. Another tradition ties the name Yafet to the Hebrew word for "beauty" (*yafeh*).

Chapter 10

1   These are the family histories of Shem, Ham, and Yafet. After the flood occurred, they fathered sons and daughters.

2   Yafet's sons were named Gomer, Magog, Madai, Yavan, Tuval, Mesheq, and Tiras.[1]

3   Gomer's sons were named Ashkenaz, Rifat, and Togarmah.

4   Yavan's sons were named Elisha, Tarshish, Kittim, and Dodanim.

5   Their clans settled in island-nations, each in its respective area. Each clan developed its own language, specific to its given nation.

6   Ham's sons were named Cush, Mitzrayim, Put, and Canaan.

7   Cush's sons were named Sava, Havilah, Savtah, Ra'amah, and Savteka. Ra'amah's sons were Sheva and Dedan.

8   Cush also fathered Nimrod. He was a very prominent, famous man on earth.[2]

9   He was a hunter of prowess in God's presence. Because of this, the saying, "Like Nimrod, the great hunter in God's presence," was popular.

---

1. *vv.* 2–7: Later Jewish tradition identifies land areas with these clans. For example, *Ashkenaz* is the ancient Hebrew name for Germany, *Tarshish* for Iberia, *Kittim* for some of the Greek Isles, *Cush* for Ethiopia/Sudan, *Mitzrayim* for Egypt, and *Put* for Libya. These identifications may be more ethnically oriented than geographically accurate land areas. However, it is of note that these ancient Hebrew names took on understood areas, especially in Egypt, Libya, Ethiopia, and the Greek Isles.

2. *v.*8: "Prominent man," the Hebrew word *gibbor*, may also be translated as "warrior." He was both a prominent military and political figure (see *v.* 10). Nimrod was identified in rabbinic thought as the leader of the rebellion that culminated in the building of the Tower of Babel (see text of Bereshit chapter 11). *v.* 10 identifies him as king of the area of Shinar, which is where the Tower was built. The Talmud informs us: ". . . why is his name called Nimrod? Because he led the entire world in rebellion, for the sake of him and his (own) kingdom. . . ." (Eruvin 53a, author's translation; accessed from http://www.e-daf .com/index.asp). The root of Nimrod's name in Hebrew (m-r-d; i.e. the letters *mem, resh,* and *daled*) is the verbal root "to rebel." Thus, the linguistic connection to the point made in Eruvim 53a is strong).

10 This was the time of the beginning of his kingdom, which included the areas of Bavel, Erek, Akad, and Kalanah, in the land of Shinar.[3]

11 Ashur came from this land, and he built Nineveh, Rehovot, Ir, and Kallah;

12 as well as Resen, which laid between Nineveh and Kallah. It was a big city.

13 And Mitzrayim fathered Ludim, Anamim, Lehavim, and Naftuchim;

14 as well as Kasluchim (from whom the Philistines descended), and Kaftorim;

15 Canaan fathered his first-born, Sidon, and then Chet;[4]

16 as well as Hayvusi, Ha'emori, and Hagirgasi,[5]

17 and Hachivi, Ha'arqi, and Hasini, [6]

18 then Ha'arvadi, Hatsmari, Hachamati, and Acher. These Canaanite clans also spread out to settle other areas.

19 Consequently, the Canaanite clans had their borders from Sidon in Bo'akah to Gerarah up to Gaza in Bo'akah, then toward Sodom, Gomorrah, Adamah, and Zevo'im, up to Lasha.

20 These are Ham's descendants, including their clans and languages, by their geographic areas.

---

3. vv. 10–11: In later Hebrew, the name *Bavel* became the name for Babylon and *Ashur* for Assyria; Nineveh was the name of the prominent city in this area.

4. v.15: Later, *Sidon* was the Hebrew name for the port city in Lebanon. *Chet* was later Hebrew for the patriarch of the Hittite nation.

5. v. 16: These three names may refer to later Canaanite kingdoms, specifically the Jebusites, Amorites and Girgasites. Thus, the text may be telling us that Canaan was the progenitor of these Canaanite nations. On the other hand, the text may be referring to specific persons who were fathered by Canaan, whose descendants named their nations after them. That is, they named their clans, settlements, or lands after their patriarchs, much as Washington, D.C., is named after America's "founding father," George Washington. Another possibility is that the Jewish people identified these nations with specific founders according to the Bereshit text, and so gave names to these nations. If that is the case, the scribes who wrote down the book of Bereshit were reporting Jewish oral tradition on the background of these clans.

6. v. 17: The Hivites may be descendants of Hachivi, their progenitor.

21 As well, Shem, the elder brother of Yafet, fathered children. He is the patriarch of the clans of Ever.[7]

22 The sons of Shem were named Elam, Ashur, Arpakshad, Lud, and Aram.

23 The sons of Aram were Utz, Chul, Geter, and Mash.

24 And Arpakshad fathered Shelach, who fathered Ever.

25 Ever had two sons whom he fathered. The name of the one was Peleg, because during his time the earth was split apart. His brother was Yaqtan.[8]

26 Yaqtan fathered Almodad, Shalef, Chatzarmavet, and Yarach,

27 as well as Hadoram, Uzal, and Diqlah,

28 Oval, Avima'el, and Sheva;

29 Ofir, Chavilah, and Yovav. They were all the sons of Yoqtan.

30 Their territory stretched from Masa-Bo'akah toward Sefarah, by the eastern mountain.

31 These were Shem's sons, including their clans and languages, by their geographic areas.

32 This was the family tree of Noah's sons according to their clans. From them the nations of the world were formed, after the great flood.

7. *v.* 21: I follow the Targum in my translation, which renders the Hebrew as telling us that Shem is the elder brother of Yafet. The NIV translation does the opposite. The Hebrew is a bit vague, but I believe is best understood as I have translated it.

8. *v.* 25: The word *peleg* in Hebrew means to "split off from" or to "separate." It is interesting to speculate what it means to have the earth "split apart." I surmise that either the physical earth was changed by geological phenomena (such as continental drift; i.e. the earth's plates moving to split land off from continents) or that this denotes a political, "religious" and social upheaval among the emerging clans or nations. The meaning of the Hebrew word "*ha'aretz*" is crucial to a proper understanding of this verse. That being said, this word is hard to define, as it can mean either the physical planet, or specifically the Land of Israel, or mankind itself.

Chapter 11

1   All mankind spoke one language, and had the same vocabulary.[1]

2   In their travels from the east, they found a valley in the land of Shinar, and lived there.

3   People said to each other, "Let's make bricks in a furnace." So they used bricks instead of stone, and clay for mortar.

4   They further said, "Let's build a city for ourselves, with a tower whose top reaches up to the sky. By doing this, we can become great and independent, so that we won't be spread across the earth."[2]

5   Then God came down to see the city and the tower that men had built.

---

1. 1v. 1: Although it is impossible to determine what language this may have been, the development of human language groups from one older, single language is a known feature of human history. Proto-Semitic is an example of this phenomenon. Scholars have identified this language as the possible single source tongue for all Semitic languages (Hebrew, Arabic, Aramaic, Syriac, Akkadian, etc.). I refer the reader to a short, descriptive article on Proto-Semitic, entitled "Proto-Semitic Language and Culture" (www.bartleby.com/61/10.html), as well as the scholarly reference work, *A Proto-Semitic Grammar and Textbook* by H. J. Shem, Winged Bull Press, 2006, for more intense study. Additionally, the idea of uniting mankind as one and then trying to build a utopian world is a theme that occurs throughout Jewish history (with Jewish civilization, usually, the victim of such a plot). This is the first historic recollection of such a plan. The book of Maccabees from the 1st century BC records another one (when the Seleucid Empire attempted to unite the Levant as "one people," including trying to subdue Israel and incorporate it into a Seleucid-Hellenist utopian empire). In the 1st and 2nd centuries, the Roman Empire attempted to do the same by subduing Israel during the *Pax Romana*, while making Jerusalem *judenrein*. In recent history, the Nazis did the same, trying to unify Europe in an Aryan-led racist "utopian" society, while attempting genocide against European Jewry. The theme of international, unifying plots has a negative connotation to it in Jewish history. I interpret the description of this one in chapter 11 in the same manner.

2. v. 4: Ziggurats are ancient buildings that are similar to this description. The remains of thirty-two ziggurats have been found in modern day Iraq and Iran, some dating from the 4th millennium BC. It was believed that deities inhabited them. Made of baked bricks, they had a pyramidal structure.

6 And God said, "So, they are united and everyone has one common language. They have already begun to work together, and now they won't hold themselves back from anything that they conceive of doing.

7 Let's go down there and scramble their speech, so that no one will understand another's language."

8 Then God scattered them from there throughout the entire earth, and they abandoned their building of that city.

9 Because of this, the city's name was called Bavel, since it was there that God scrambled the language of mankind, and from there God scattered them throughout the earth.[3]

10 This is the family history of Shem: Shem was 100 years old when he fathered Arpakshad, two years after the great flood.

11 Shem lived another 500 years after he fathered Arpakshad, and he fathered other sons and daughters.

12 Arpakshad was 35 years old when he fathered Shelach.

13 Arpakshad lived another 403 years after he fathered Shelach, and he fathered other sons and daughters.

14 Shelach was 30 years old when he fathered Ever.

15 Shelach lived another 403 years after he fathered Ever, and he fathered other sons and daughters.

16 Ever was 34 years old when he fathered Peleg.

17 Ever lived another 430 years after he fathered Peleg, and he fathered other sons and daughters.

18 Peleg was 30 years old when he fathered Re'u.

19 Peleg lived another 290 years after he fathered Re'u, and he fathered other sons and daughters.

---

3. *v. 9:* "Bavel" is a play on the world *balal*, which is an ancient Hebrew onomatopoeia for the sound of unintelligible babble. In later Semitic linguistics, *bab* is a gate (as it is in modern Arabic) and el refers to a deity; thus the name may be a later Hebrew designation for the "entryway" or "gate" to heaven (or God), which fits the context well. Some scholars believe that this particular tower was a seven-floor high ziggurat with a temple dedicated to the idol Marduk sitting at the very top.

20 Re'u was 32 years old when he fathered Serug.

21 Re'u lived another 207 years after he fathered Serug, and he fathered other sons and daughters.

22 Serug was 30 years old when he fathered Nachor.

23 Serug lived another 200 years after he fathered Nachor, and he fathered other sons and daughters.

24 Nachor was 29 years old when he fathered Terach.

25 Nachor lived another 119 years after he fathered Terach, and he fathered other sons and daughters.

26 Terach was 70 years old when he fathered Avram, then Nachor and then Haran.

27 This is Terach's family history: Terach fathered Avram, Nachor, and Haran. Haran fathered Lot.

28 Haran died in Ur, his hometown in the Kasdim region, during the lifetime of Terach, his father.[4]

29 Avram and Nachor both married. Avram's wife was named Sarai, and Nachor's wife was Milkah, who along with her sister Yiskah were Haran's daughters.

30 Sarai was infertile, and could not have children.

31 Terach then took his son Avram along with his daughter-in-law Sarai, who was Avram's wife, as well as Lot his grandson, who was born to his son Haran. They arrived at Charan and settled there.

32 Terach lived to be 205 years old, and finally he died at Charan.

---

4. *vv.* 28 *and* 31: The name Haran (Avraham's brother) has a soft 'h' pronounced as the first sound of the name, as it begins with the Hebrew letter "he" (equivalent to an English letter h). The site Charan has a harder "ch" sound at its beginning, as it begins with the Hebrew letter "chet." Thus, Terach did not name this site after his deceased son.

Chapter 12

1   God spoke to Avram and said, "'Go already, leave your land, your homeland, and your father's household, and go to the Land that I will show you. [1]

2   I am going to make you into a great nation. I am going to give you reason to bow your knees in thanksgiving (to God). I will make your reputation well known. You will give reason for people to bow their knees in thanksgiving (to God).[2]

3   I will give people who help you a reason to bow their knees in thanksgiving; however, those who oppose you, I will utterly curse. Through your life all peoples of the world will have reason to bow their knees in thanksgiving (to God)."

4   Avram went just as God instructed him, and Lot went with him. Avram was seventy-five years old when he departed from Charan.

5   Avram took his wife Sarai, Lot his nephew and all of their goods and servants that they had acquired in Charan. They left for the land of Canaan, and they eventually arrived in the land of Canaan.

6   Then Avram traveled in the Land until he arrived at Shechem, to the place of the oak trees of Moreh. Canaanites were then numerous in the Land.[3]

---

1. *v.1*: This verse displays a sense of urgency in the language used. A very colloquially accurate way to translate the given Hebrew phrase, *lek leka* may be, "Get the heck out of . . . !" God here calls Avram to hurriedly leave his family roots, both physically and spiritually.

2. *v. 2*: The Hebrew word for "blessing" (*berakah*) derives from the word for an anatomical knee. Literally, to "receive a blessing" or to "be a blessing" involved the word "knee" in ancient Hebrew. So I have translated this concept here in an idiomatic fashion. That is, one bows his knee in thanksgiving to God when he is given a reason to do so; thus, the concept of blessing entails a physical response to God by the recipient (namely, the bending of the knees).

3. The "oak trees of Mamre" (my translation) is also translated as "plains of Mamre" (Targum Onkelos), "oracle giving oak" (JPS) and "teacher tree"(Forward Magazine). For a discussion of the nuances of each translation, I refer the reader to "Back to Mamre" by Philologos, found at: http://www.forward.com/articles/12049/.

7   God appeared to Avram and said, "I give this Land to your descendants." So he built an altar to worship God, Who appeared to him.

8   He went on from there in the direction of the hilly land to the east of BethEl. He pitched his tent where BethEl was to the west, and Ai was to the east. Then he built an altar to God, and called on God's name.

9   Avram then traveled onward, into the Negev Desert.

10 There was a famine in the Land, so Avram went down to Egypt to live there, because this famine in the Land was quite severe.

11 When Avram approached the Egyptian border, he said to his wife, Sarai, "Look, you're really a beautiful woman.[4]

12 When the Egyptians see you and tell each other that you are my wife, they will kill me but spare you.

13 So say that you are my sister. That way you will insure that things will go well for me, and that I'll stay alive."

14 When Avram reached the Egyptian frontier, the Egyptians thought that Sarai was quite stunning.

15 Officials of the pharaoh of Egypt saw Sarai, and they spoke highly of her to the pharaoh. She was then taken to the Pharaoh's palace.

16 Things went well for Avram because of her. He was given sheep, cattle, male and female donkeys, male and female servants, and camels.

17 But God struck Pharaoh and his palace with many serious diseases because of what happened to Sarai, the wife of Avram.

18 Then Pharaoh summoned Avram, and asked, "What did you do to me? Why didn't you tell me that she is your wife?

19 Why did you say that she is your sister? So I took her for my wife, and now I find out that she's already your wife! Take her and get out of here!"

20 Pharaoh summoned his servants, and they escorted him and his wife out, along with all of their possessions.

---

4. *vv.* 11–14: Jewish tradition ascribes great beauty to Sarah, commenting on this section of the biblical text: "The rabbis taught: 'There were four beautiful women in the world: Sarah, Rahab, Abigail and Esther'" (Megillah 15a).

Chapter 13

1 Avram came up out of Egypt along with his wife and his entire house-hold, including Lot, and went to the Negev Desert.

2 Avram was overloaded with animals, silver and gold.

3 He then went traveling from the Negev Desert to Bet-El, to the very place where in the past he had put up his tent, between Bet-El and Ai,

4 to the place where he had once made an altar, where he called on the name of God.

5 Lot also went with Avram, and he also owned sheep, cattle, and tents.

6 But the Land was not able to sustain both of them, as they had so much property between the two of them that they could not live together.

7 A quarrel broke out between the shepherds of Avram's herds and the shepherds of Lot's herds. The Canaanites and the Perizzites were firmly entrenched in the Land at that time.

8 Then Avram said to Lot, "Let's not have a quarrel between the two of us, or between our shepherds, because we are close family.

9 Isn't all the Land right here, for you to choose from? Please separate from me. If you choose to go to the left, I will go to the right; and if to the right, I will go to the left."

10 Lot viewed the area, and saw the southern Jordan Valley, that it was plush and like the garden of God. The area leading to So'ar was similar to Egypt. This occurred before the destruction of Sodom and Gomorrah. [1]

11 So Lot chose the entire southern Jordan Valley, and he then traveled east to get there. The family then became physically divided.

---

1. *v.* 10: An allusion to the garden of Eden is being made by the phrase "garden of God." This beautiful and lush area made Lot think that the southern Jordan Valley region was a virtual paradise, and was akin to both the garden of Eden and the fertile Egyptian delta.

12 Avram settled in the land of Canaan, and Lot settled in the area of the cities of the Valley, finally living in Sodom.

13 The citizens of Sodom were wicked people who brazenly broke God's Torah.[2]

14 So God spoke to Avram after he and Lot parted company, saying, "'From where you are, take a look towards the north, then towards the south, then to the east, and to the west,

15 because I will give you and your descendants all the Land that you see, forever.[3]

16 I will also make your descendants like the dust of the ground, immeasurable. If the amount of dust on the ground could be measured, only then could your descendants be counted.

17 Get up and walk in the Land, see its length and its breadth, because I will give all of it to you."

18 Avram moved his tents, and came to live by the oaks of Mamre (also known as Hevron). He built an altar there to worship God. [4]

2. 2v. 13: Since I define "sin" as transgressing the Torah, I have translated the Hebrew word *chet* and its derivatives in that light. Here the word is *chatta'im*, and my translation brings to light what their activities did—they went against God's Torah (His instructions on how to live). Even though the Written Torah had not yet been received on Mt. Sinai by Moses and his generation, there were still certain *mitzvot* (instructions) that God had instructed to Noah.

3. 3v. 15: The Hebrew is very poetic and beautiful here, as it describes the physical geography of the Land. God specifically instructs Avram to look north, then toward the Negev desert, afterward toward the area of the garden of Eden, then toward the Sea (the Mediterranean). I would love to translate this verse in this fashion, however to render it into more idiomatic English, I chose to use the four directions in lieu of the more poetic Hebrew physical, land geographic indicators.

4. 4v. 18: While the literal Hebrew says that he built an altar "to God," this is best understood as a phrase of purpose; thus, throughout my translation, I have rendered this phrase as "to worship God," which best fits the context of the narrative.

Chapter 14

1   During their reigns, kings Amrafel of Shinar, Ariok of Elasar, Kedarla'omer of Elam, and Tidal of an unnamed foreign nation,

2   warred against Bera, king of Sodom, Birsha, king of Gomorrah, Shinav, king of Admah, Shemever, king of Zevoi'im, and King Bela of So'ar.

3   They joined forces and went to the Valley of Haseddim, that is, the Dead Sea.

4   For twelve years these kings served Kedarla'omer, but in the thirteenth year they rebelled.

5   So in the fourteenth year, Kedarla'omer and his allied kings came and conquered the Refa'im in Ashterot Karnayim, the nomads of Ham, and threatening forces in Shaveh-Kiratayim,

6   as well as the mountain peoples of Seir, all the way to Paran Palm, the site in the wilderness.

7   Then they returned and came to Mishpat Spring, also known as Kadesh. They invaded the entire Amalekite plain, as well as the Amorite one, that is located in Chatseson-Tamar.

8   Then the kings of Sodom, Gomorrah, Admah, Zevo'im and King Bela of So'ar formed a military front to wage war in the Valley of Seddim,

9   against King Kedarla'omer of Elam, Tidal of the unnamed nation, Amrafel of Shinar and Ariok of Elasar; four kings went up against five kings.

10   The Valley of Hassedim had many mud sinkholes in it. The kings of Sodom and Gomorrah were routed there, and fell there. The survivors fled into the hilly region.

11   All possessions from Sodom and Gomorrah were taken as booty, as well as all foodstuffs. Then they (the victorious kings) left.

12   They kidnapped Avram's nephew Lot, and took his possessions, because he lived in Sodom.

13 An escapee came and told Avram the Hebrew (who lived by the oak trees of Mamre the Amorite, who was the brother of Eshkol and Anar). They were all allies of Avram.

14 So Avram heard that his close family member had been captured. He then outfitted and equipped 318 young men of his clan and pursued (the four kings) till Dan.

15 At night, Avram divided up his men into groups, and struck his enemies, pursuing them to Chovah, which is north of Damascus. [1]

16 He recovered all the plundered property, as well as Lot his nephew and his personal property, and finally the women and other kidnapped persons.

17 After he returned from defeating Kedarla'omer and the allied kings, the king of Sodom came to meet him at the Valley of Shaveh, that is, the Valley of the King.[2]

18 Then Malki-sedek, the king of Shalem, brought out bread and wine. He was a priest of the Most High God.[3]

19 So he pronounced a blessing for him, saying, "Blessed is Avram by the Most High

---

1. *v.* 15: The word *semol*, used for "north" of Damascus can indeed mean north, and is most often taken that way; however, it may mean west of the city, if *semol* is translated "to the *left*: (westward) as it can be translated. In Hebrew, *semol* usually means "left"; in Arabic *shmol* connotes "north." Those who favor a "north" meaning for the Hebrew connect the ancient Hebrew *semol* to the Semitic word *shmol*. Because the word *tsafon* (north) existed in ancient Hebrew and is used in the book of Bereshit, I favor the translation that I used.

2. *v.* 17: Often we fail to appreciate the military leadership that Avraham displayed. For his clan (even with the help of allied kings) to track and defeat Kedarla'omer and his allied fighters was an act of bravery, skill, and prowess, needing decisive and talented leadership and strategic planning).

3. *v.* 18: The figure of Malki-sedek is written about both in the Newer Testament (book of Hebrews) and in Qumran Literature. In Qumran fragment 11Q13, Malki-sedek is a divinely empowered judge, deliverer, and the one who metes out an inheritance to the righteous. "Melchizedek . . . who will return them to what is rightfully theirs. He will proclaim to them the Jubilee, thereby releasing them from the debt of all their sins. He shall proclaim this decree in the first week of the jubilee period that follows nine jubilee periods" (taken from http://www.gnosis. org/library/commelc.htm). The book of Hebrews writes of Malki-sedek as the High Priest of a heavenly priesthood (cf. 7:15–17), who had a superior status to that of Avraham.

God, Who owns the heavens and the earth. [4]

20 And blessed is the Most High God Who protected you from your foes."
He then gave him a tenth part of everything that he had with him.

21 The king of Sodom said to Avram, "Give me the kidnapped people,
and you can keep the property."

22 Avram replied to the king of Sodom, "I have sworn to God Most High,
owner of the heavens and the earth,

23 that I won't take anything that is yours, whether a thread or a sandal
strap, so that you won't say that you made me wealthy.

24 Only what my men have eaten, and the booty that my allies who
came with me, from Aner, Eshkol and Mamre—let them take their
portion."

---

4. *v. 19*: A nice alternative reading could be, '. . . Avram will be given reasons to bow
his knee in thanks to the Most High God . . .'

Chapter 15

1 After all of these events, God's words came to Avram in a vision, saying, "Don't fear, Avram. I am your protector, and your reward will be very large."

2 Avram replied, "Lord God, what (reward) will you grant me, as I am without an heir, and the inheritor of my clan is Eliezer of Damascus."[1]

3 Avram continued, "So because You have not given me children, a household member will be my inheritor!"

4 Then God's words came to him, saying, "He won't be your inheritor. Instead, your own offspring will be your inheritor."

5 He took him outdoors, and said, "Please look at the sky, and count the number of stars if you can count them." And He added, "This is how your descendants will be."[2]

6 So he believed God, and this was counted as an act of righteousness.

7 Then He said to him, "I am God, Who took you from Ur of the Kasdim, in order to give you this Land as an inheritance."

8 He responded, "Lord God, how can I be sure that I will inherit it?"

9 So (God) said to him, "Bring a bound calf, a bound goat, and a bound ram to me. Also bring a pigeon and a pigeon chick."[3]

1. *v. 2*: Avram engages the Almighty in a conversation about the reward that is promised in v. 1.

2. *v. 5*: The Hebrew uses the revealing word *na*, which I have translated as "please." It makes
God's message here a strong yet intimate plea. He is depicted as kindly, lovingly, and even politely explaining the fuller situation to Avram, much as a father would allay his son's fears while explaining a situation to him.

3. *v. 9*: The word *meshulash* is translated by all translators as "three years old." However, *meshulash* could refer to an animal being bound by three ropes for carrying purposes (while still alive, before being butchered; that is, "hogtied"). In modern Hebrew, *meshulash* refers to a triangle, thus giving a graphic image of the idea that the animal is being tied to where it resembled a triangular shape. I am not opposing the usual translation, but offering this as a possible alternative translation. Thus, I translated the verse in this alternative manner.

10 He took all of these, and butchered them in half, putting each piece next to the other. But he did not slaughter the birds.

11 Vultures swooped down on the carcasses, so Avram drove them off.

12 When evening came, Avram fell into a deep sleep, when he experienced terror and great darkness.

13 Then He said to Avram, "Understand that your descendants will definitely live in a foreign land that is not theirs, and they will be enslaved and tortured for four hundred years.[4]

14 Yet I will judge the nation that enslaves them. Immediately afterward, they (Avram's descendants) will leave there with many possessions.

15 And you are going to die in peace. You will buried when you are quite elderly.

16 It will be in the fourth generation that they will return here, as the transgressions of the Amorites are not going to be finished before then."

17 The sun had already set, and darkness came. A smoking oven and a fiery torch appeared, with the torch moving between the pieces.

18 On that day, God made a covenant with Avram, saying, "I have given this very Land to your descendants, from the river of Egypt, to the Great River, the Euphrates.

19 This includes the area of the Kenites, the Kenizites and the Kadmonites;

20 the Hittites, the Perizites and the Refa'im;

21 the Amorites, the Canaanites, the Girgashites, and the Jebusites."

---

4. *vv.* 13–14: Although Jewish thought does not develop the tension between predestination and free choice that the later Christian world did, these verses definitely become a blueprint of destiny for the remainder of the book of Bereshit and for the book of Exodus.

Chapter 16

1   Avram's wife, Sarai, had not borne him children. She had a female servant, an Egyptian named Hagar.

2   So Sarai told Avram, "Please, look! God has made me unable to give birth. Please have sexual relations with my servant. Maybe I can build a family through her." Avram gave heed to Sarai's plea.

3   Then Sarai, Avram's wife, took Hagar, her Egyptian servant and gave her to Avram in order to have sexual relations. This happened when Avram had lived ten years in the land of Canaan. [1]1

4   So he had relations with Hagar, who became pregnant. When it was clear that she was pregnant, she then despised her guardian (Sarai).

5   Sarai said to Avram, "I've had it with what you did! I put my servant in your embrace, she gets pregnant, and now she despises me! God will judge between you and me!"

6   Avram replied to Sarai, "Look, you have authority over your own servant. Do to her whatever you want." So Sarai treated her poorly, and she fled.

7   An angel of God found her at a water spring in the wilderness, on the road to Shur.

8   So he said to Hagar, Sarai's servant, "Where did you come from? Where are you going?" She replied, "I am running away from Sarai, my guardian."

9   The angel of God said to her, "Return to your guardian, and take whatever consequences that she gives you."

10 The angel further said to her, "God will greatly increase your descendants so that it will be impossible to count them."

---

1. *v.* 3: One may surmise that Hagar was acquired from Avram and Sarai's time in Egypt (cf. 12.10, 16).

11 Again the angel of God told her, "'See, you are pregnant, and you will have a son and call his name Ishmael, because God has listened to your sorrows.[2]

12 "He will be a wild man, in conflict with everyone around him, yet he will live in close proximity to his relatives."

13 She called God, Who passed on this message to her, by the name, "You are the Almighty Who sees me," and she further stated, "Did I really see the One Who sees me?"

14 Therefore, the name of this well was called "The well of the Living Watchman," that is between Kadesh and Bared.

15 Hagar gave birth to a son for Avram, and Avram named his son that Hagar had given him Ishmael.

16 Avram was eighty-six years old when Hagar gave birth to his son Ishmael.

---

2. *v.*11: *Ishmael* is a derivative of the Hebrew root *shma* (to hear), so they sound similar.

Chapter 17

1   When Avram was ninety-nine years old, God appeared to him. He (God) said to him, "I am Almighty God. Walk yourself before me, and be exactly who I created you to be.[1]

2   And I will pass on my covenant from me to you; I will make your descendants very, very numerous."[2]

3   So Avram fell on his face, and God spoke to him, saying,

4   "Here, my very covenant is yours; you will be a father to many nations.

5   Your name will no longer be Avram. Your name is Avraham, because I am making you a father to many nations.

6   I will make you very, very fruitful, expanding you into nations. Kings will come from you.

---

1. *v*.1: To paraphrase this instruction, "Live your life righteously before Me, and be whole". This is a valid way of understanding what God tells Avram. God here gives Avraham the responsibility to live correctly and to become the person who God wanted him to be.

2. *v.* 5: "Avraham" means "father of many people." One viewpoint in the Talmud explains the significance of his name change as follows: "Avram, he is Avraham. At first he became a father to Aram (thus his name, Av [Hebrew for "father"]-ram [i.e., Hebrew for "Aram"]). Finally, he became a father to the entire world (thus his name, Av [father]-raham [many people]). Sarai, she is Sarah. At first she became a princess to her own people ("Sarai"), and finally she became ("Sarah"), a princess to the entire world" (Berakhot 13a, author's translation; accessed from http://e-daf.com/index.asp). Another Talmudic explanation on the name changes is as follows: ". . . Rabbi Johanan said in the name of Rabbi Jose ben Zimra: 'Whence do we know that there are abbreviated letters in the Scriptures? As it is written [in Gen. 17. 5]: *Khi Ab Hamaun Goyim Nsathicha* (For the father of a multitude of nations have I made thee). In the word *Ab* the (first letter) Aleph is the abbreviation of *Ab*—father, and the (second letter) *Beth* stands for *bachur*—selected; *Hamaun* stands for *haviv*—lovely, *Melech*—king, *vathig*—modest, *neamon*—upright. All this I have made thee among the nations'" (Shabbat 105a, accessed from: http://www .jewishvirtuallibrary.org/jsource/Talmud/ shabbat12.html).

Rabbi Yohanan here teaches that the very Hebrew words of our text use an acronym that hint at the fuller meaning of Avram's new name, Avraham. To Yohanan, the very name Avraham refers to him being a chosen, beloved, modest, and upright king to the world.

7   So I will establish my covenant between me, you, and your descendants who come after you in their generations. It is an eternal covenant, in which I will be your God, and that of your descendants who come after you.

8   I have given Canaan, the land of your residence, to you and to your descendants after you as an eternal inheritance. I will be their God."

9   Then God said to Avraham, "You must keep my covenant, both you and your descendants after you in their generations.

10   This is my covenant between you and I, and your descendants after you that you must keep—circumcise every male.

11   This will be the sign of my covenant between you and I, when your uncircumcised body is circumcised.

12   Every single boy in your generation is to be circumcised when he is eight days old, both a boy born in your home, and every foreign boy who is born and bought with money, who is not your physical descendant.

13   You must circumcise a boy born in your home, as well as one who is bought with money. My covenant will be evidenced in your physical body as an everlasting covenant.

14   Any boy who is not physically circumcised will be exiled from his people, for my covenant is being violated."

15   Then God spoke to Avraham: "Don't call your wife Sarai by the name Sarai, because Sarah is now her name.

16   I will give her reasons to bow her knee in thanks, and also I will give you a son through her. I will bless her and kings of nations will come through her lineage."

17   Then Avraham prostrated himself in worship, but he laughed, and thought, "Can a son be born to a hundred-year-old? And can Sarah, who is ninety years old, give birth?"

18   So Avraham said to God, "May Ishma'el live long before You!"

But God replied, "But Sarah your wife will give birth to a son for you, and you will name him Isaac. I will continue My covenant with him as an eternal covenant, and to his descendants.[3]

19 I have heard your plea concerning Ishmaʾel, and I will bless him, making him fruitful and very, very numerous. Twelve rulers will come through his lineage, and I will make his descendants a great people.

20 But it is with Isaac, whom Sarah will bear for you at this very time next year, that I will continue my covenant."

21 Then He ended conversing with him, after which God left Avraham's presence.

22 So Avraham took his son Ishmaʾel, along with every single male of Avraham's clan—those who were born into his clan or bought with his money. And he circumcised their foreskins on that very day, just as God instructed him to do.

23 And Avraham was ninety-nine years old when his uncircumcised flesh was circumcised.

24 Ishmaʾel his son was thirteen years old when his uncircumcised flesh was circumcised.

25 Actually, on the very same day Avraham was circumcised along with Ishmaʾel his son.

26 So, all the males of his clan, both the ones born and the ones bought with money from foreigners, were circumcised along with him.

---

3. *v. 19:* The Hebrew name for Isaac is "Yitzhak" and it is a word play on the word "laugh" (cf. 17.17, *vayitzhak*).

Chapter 18

1   Afterward, God appeared to him by the oak trees of Mamre, while he was sitting in the entryway to his tent in the heat of the day.

2   He looked up and suddenly there were three men standing straight ahead of him. He saw them, got up from his tent's entry, and ran to greet them, then fell prostrate before them.

3   Then he spoke, "Gentlemen, please do me a favor, and don't leave.

4   A little bit of water will be brought, and you can wash your feet, then stay to rest under the trees.

5   I'll bring you some bread, and you can eat to your heart's content. Afterward, feel free to leave. But now you are with me, so let me serve you." They replied, "Okay, do as you say."

6   So Avraham rushed into the tent, to Sarah, and said, "Hurry and knead three seahs of flour and make semolina cakes."

7   Avraham then hurried to his cattle, took one of them that was young and of high quality, and gave it to a young servant, who rushed to prepare it.

8   He then took butter, milk, and the meat that he had prepared and gave it to them. They ate it while he stood by them under the trees.

9   Then they asked him, "Where is Sarah your wife?" He responded, "Here, in the tent."

10 So he said, "I will again return to you during this same season, and Sarah your wife will have a son." Sarah was listening from the tent entry.[1]

---

1. *v.* 10: The Hebrew phrase used in this verse, *ka'et chayah*, is most often translated as "during the same season, in the next year." "The . . . phrase, 'when the season comes around,' (*ka'et chayah*) is literally 'at the time (or season) of life.' It is a reference to the new year in the spring, in the month of Abib or Nisan (see Exodus 12:2)", http://unitedisrael .org/blog/ 2009/03/26/ happy-new-year-the-times-and-the-seasons/. In the Talmud, we are told that Isaac was born at Passover, in the springtime, and the word "'*et*" (time, season) is translated as "festival time" (probably referring to a Leviticus chapter 23 "*mo'ed*," or festival/holyday time). "Isaac was born in Nissan. Whence do we know this? It is writ-

11 But Avraham and Sarah were old and advanced in age. Sarah could no longer bear children.

12 Then Sarah laughed to herself, saying, "It is after my time (to bear children), so how can I experience this delight? Plus, my husband is old."

13 God said to Avraham, "Why did Sarah laugh, and say, 'Will I really give birth? I'm too old.'

14 Is there any thing that is too wonderful for God? At this very time next year I will return to you, and Sarah will have a son."

15 But Sarah denied it, and said, "I didn't laugh," because she was afraid. And He said, "But you indeed did laugh."

16 The men got up to leave, and they looked out toward Sodom. Avraham escorted them away, seeing them off.

17 Afterwards, God said, "Should I conceal from Avraham what I am about to do?

18 After all, Avraham will be a great and strong nation, and all nations of the world will be given a reason to bow their knees in thanks because of him.

19 I have appointed him to instruct both his descendants and his clan to carefully guard the halakah of God—to carry out righteousness and justice, so that God will bring about all that has been promised about Avraham."[2]

20 Then God said, "The outcry against Sodom and Gomorrah is very intense; their breaking of the Torah is quite serious.[3]

---

ten (Bereshit 18.24): "At the next festival I will return to thee, and Sarah will have a son" (Rosh Hashanah 16a, taken from: http://www.jewishvirtuallibrary.org/jsource/Talmud/rh1.html). So, Passover is identified as the "*et chayah*," that is, the season and time being referred to here.

2. v. 19: Although it is God speaking in this verse, He is referred to twice in the third person. In doing this, the Torah is using a literary device and means of speaking that is part of Hebrew poetic and narrative literature. 'Halakah' is Hebrew for the legal requirements of carrying out God's instructions (His Torah). It constitutes the way to follow God. It is an accurately descriptive word for what is being conveyed in this verse.

3. v. 20: Although a modern site named Sodom exists in today's modern Israel, it is not identified as the site from this narrative. My former archaeology professor at Valparaiso University, Dr. Walter Rast, identified Sodom and Gomorrah as an area that he and a colleague of his, Dr. Thomas Schaub, found in the early 1970s. They identified it

21 I'll go down to see about these cries that have come to me, to find out if they have done what they are accused of doing. If not, I will find out."

22 So the men left there, and they went toward Sodom, while Avraham still stood in front of

God.

23 Avraham approached Him, and said, "Will you destroy the righteous along with the wicked?

24 Let's say there are fifty righteous people in the city; will you destroy it? Won't you spare the place because of the fifty righteous people in its midst?[4]

25 May it be forbidden! You can't do this, to kill the righteous along with the wicked. Are the righteous the same as the wicked? May it be forbidden! The Judge of the world can't do this kind of judging!"

26 God then replied, "If I find fifty righteous people in the city of Sodom, then I'll spare the entire place on their account."

27 Avraham then answered, saying, "Please be patient, because I have dared to continue speaking to my Lord, and I am but dust and ashes.

28 If by chance there are five people less than fifty righteous people, will You destroy the entire city because of a lack of five people?" And He replied, "I won't destroy it if I find forty-five (righteous people) there."

29 He dared again to speak to Him, saying, "What if there are forty righteous people?" So He answered, "I won't destroy it due to the merit of these forty."

30 So he said, "Please, my Lord, don't get mad, but allow me to speak. What if there are thirty righteous people?" So He answered, "I won't destroy it if I find thirty righteous people there."

---

as the sites of Bab ed-Dra and Numeira (in modern day Jordan).

4. *vv.* 24–33: I cannot stress how awesome and rare this conversation is among the narratives of the Torah, due to its intimacy between man and God. In addition, the Hebrew portrays Avraham as being both very polite yet extremely bold to press his case in the very presence of Almighty God. This is "holy *chutzpah*" (Hebrew and Yiddish for "intestinal fortitude") that portrays God as a very merciful benefactor, and One to whom His servants can talk to about intimate, troubling matters. This pattern of relationship with the Avot (the Patriarchs) is established early in the narratives of the Torah.

31 So he replied, "Please be patient, since I dare to speak again to my Lord. What if twenty righteous people are found there?" And He replied, "I won't destroy it due to the merit of these twenty."

32 And then he said, "Please, my Lord, don't be mad, but allow me to speak just one more time. What if ten righteous people are there?" He said, "I won't destroy it due to the merit of these ten."

33 So God finished speaking to Avraham, and then He left, while Avraham returned to his home.

Chapter 19

1   The two angelic messengers came to Sodom in the evening. Lot was sitting in the gate of Sodom, and Lot saw (them). So he rose up to meet them, and prostrated himself to the ground.

2   Then he said, "Please, sirs, come to your servant's home and stay overnight. You can also wash your feet. When morning comes, you can then go on your way." They responded, "No, we'll sleep in the street."

3   But he practically begged them, and they agreed to come with him. They arrived at his home, and he made a sumptuous meal for them, with baked unleavened bread, which they ate.[1]

4   However, before they went to sleep, all the men of the city of Sodom, from youths to the elderly, surrounded (Lot's) home. Everyone was there.

5   They called out to Lot, and said to him, "Where are the men that came to your home this evening? Bring them outside to us, so we can sexually abuse them."

6   Then Lot went outside to them and shut the door behind him.

7   He said, "My brothers, please don't carry out such an evil act.

8   Look, I have two daughters that are virgins. I'll bring them out and you can do whatever you'd like to them. Just don't do anything to these men, because they have sought protection under my roof."[2]

9   They replied, "Get out of the way!" Then they said, "This guy came to us to live here, and now he is judging us? We'll get you, too, right after them!" So they pushed forward forcefully against Lot, till they were getting close to breaking down the door.[3]

---

1. *v. 3*: Lot literally made *matza* (unleavened bread) for his guests. This would have saved a few minutes of time.

2. *v. 8*: In the ancient Middle East, and even today among the Bedouins, the protection of one's guests is a serious obligation. The Torah does not justify Lot's alternative offer, but we do see how serious a matter of honor it was to him to insure that his guests were safe and sound.

3. *v. 9*: Lot is depicted in this comment as an outsider to the ways of Sodom, and as one who has no right to moralize to them.

10 The guests grabbed Lot and pulled him to them inside his home. They also shut the door.

11 They then struck the men who were outside the door of the home with blindness, from the youngest to the oldest, so that they failed to find the entrance.

12 So the guests said to Lot, "Who else is here? Do you have a son-in-law, or sons, or other daughters? Take everything that you have in this city, and get out of this place,

13 because we are going to destroy this place. There is a great outcry (from Sodom) that reached God's very presence. So it is God Who sent us to destroy it."

14 Lot left in order to speak to his future sons-in-law, who were engaged to his daughters. He said, "Get up, leave this place because God will destroy the city." His future sons-in-law thought this was a joke.

15 When dawn came, the messenger angels implored Lot, saying, "Get up, take your wife and your two daughters who are with you, so you won't be destroyed because of the crimes of the city."

16 But he stalled for time, so the two men grabbed him and his wife by the hand. And they took the hands of his two daughters, because God had mercy on him. So they took him outside of the city, saving him.

17 As they were bringing them out of the city, (a messenger angel) said, "Flee for your life! Don't look back, and don't stop anywhere in the area! Flee to the hills or you will be destroyed!"[4]

18 Then Lot said to them, "No, please, sirs!

19 You've really had mercy on me. So do me a favor like you did when you saved my life. I can't make it to the hills because the destruction will overtake us on the way and I'll die.

20 Look, there is a town to run to that is close by. It's small-sized; please, I can flee there. It's small, but can't it give shelter and save my life?"

---

4. *v.* 17: The word *kikar* is translated here as "area," though I believe it specifically refers to the four-town region of Sodom, Gomorrah, Admah, and Zevo'im, which all perished in the destruction. In other words, this may have been a command not to stop for shelter in one of the area's three towns (i.e., Gomorrah. Admah, and Zevo'im). Zo'ar was the one town in the area that was spared (see *v.* 19).

21 He replied to him, "Alright, I will, as well, agree to this request, and I won't overthrow this town that you are speaking about.

22 But hurry, run there, because I can't do anything until you arrive there." And so the name of the town was called "Zo'ar."

23 When the sun set over the Land, Lot had arrived in Zo'ar.

24 So God engulfed Sodom and Gomorrah in a sulfur and firestorm by His decree from Heaven.[5]

25 He totally demolished these cities and the entire area, with all the inhabitants of the cities, including all vegetation that was growing in the ground.

26 Lot's wife, however, had looked back and became a pile of salt.[6]

27 Avraham woke up early in the morning and went to the site where he had stood before God.[7]

28 He looked out toward the area of Sodom and Gomorrah, and toward the south Dead Sea region. As he looked, he could see thick smoke rising up from the ground. It looked like the smoke of a furnace.

5. *v.* 24: ". . . *me'et HaShem min hashamayim*" is translated in most versions as "from the sky" or "from the heavens," giving us a sense of the physical place where the firestorm originated. However, sometimes the word '*hashamayim*' can refer to the place where God exists, and the text first tells us that He is the origin of the firestorm. Thus, I prefer the notion that from "His heavenly abode," God decided (thus "decreed") this destructive firestorm. I am not saying that the more common translation is wrong; I simply prefer this alternative.

6. *v.* 26: To "become salt" may be a Hebrew idiom for being "completely destroyed." The text may be informing us that Lot's wife was "snuffed out" or "wiped out," i.e., killed. I refer the reader to the article by Weston Fields, "Salted With Fire," found at: http:/www .jerusalem perspective.com/ Default.aspxtabid=27&ArticleID=1454. Fields notes that: "The case of Lot's wife, who was destroyed when she disobeyed God's command and was turned into a 'pillar of salt,' is well known. It is probably as an allusion to this familiar incident . . . (where) Isaiah 51.6 uses the root *m-l-h* in the sense of 'destroy.'"

7. *v.* 27: In Jewish literature, this verse is used to teach us how to pray: "Rabbi Helbo taught by Rabbi Huna's authority that everyone who has a specific place for his prayers, the God of Avraham will be his helper. Avraham our father made it his practice to have a specific place (of prayer), as it is written, 'Avraham woke up early in the morning, and went to the site where he had stood before God'" (Berakhot 6b, author's translation). *v.* 28: Although the text does not literally read "the south Dead Sea region," this is the very area to which the ancient Hebrew *al panay 'eretz hakikar* (on the plain of the Land) is referring. My translation incorporates the modern geographical term.

29 God remembered Avraham when He destroyed the cities of this region by sending Lot away from the storms. Through them He decimated the cities in the area in which Lot lived.

30 Then, Lot left Zo'ar and resettled in the hills. His two daughters were with him. They were afraid to settle in Zo'ar, so he and his two daughters lived in a cave.

31 So the older daughter said to the younger one, "Our father is old, and there are no men left with whom to form families.

32 Let's get our father drunk with wine and then have sexual relations with him so that we can continue the family line."

33 They gave their father wine to drink during that very night, and indeed the oldest daughter slept with her father. He did not even know that she had entered or left his presence.

34 On the very next day, the older daughter told the younger, "I had sexual relations last night with my father. Let's get him drunk with wine tonight, too, and then you have sexual relations with him, so that our father's family line continues."

35 So she (the eldest) also got her father drunk with wine on that very night, and then the younger daughter had sexual relations with him. Again, he did not even know that she had entered or left his presence.

36 Both of Lot's daughters became pregnant by him.

37 The oldest daughter gave birth to a son, and named him Mo'av. He is known as the patriarch of the Moabite nation till today.

38 The younger daughter also gave birth to a son and named him Ben-ammi. He is known as the patriarch of the Ammonite nation till today.

Chapter 20

1   Avraham went on from there into the Negev Desert, and temporarily lived between Kadesh and Shur before he settled in Gerar.

2   Then Avraham said about Sarah his wife, "She is my sister." So Avimelek the king of Gerar sent for Sarah and took her.

3   So God came to Avimelek in a dream during the night, and said to him, "You will die because of this woman that you took, because she is a wife and has a husband."

4   As a result, Avimelek did not come near her, and he said, "Lord, will you also kill off a righteous nation?

5   Didn't he tell me that she was his sister? And didn't she also say that he was her brother? I did this innocently and without any guilt!"

6   Then God said to him in a dream, "I certainly know that you did this innocently. I also prevented you from transgressing My will, because I didn't let you touch her.

7   So now return the man's wife, because the man is a prophet. He will pray for you and you will live. If you don't return her, know that you and your entire family will definitely die!"

8   Avimelek woke up early in the morning and summoned all of his servants. He explained everything to them, and they were very fearful.

9   Then Avimelek summoned Avraham, and told him, "What have you done to us? In what way have I wronged you that you cause me and my entire kingdom to commit a great wrong? You have done things to me that should never be done!"

10   Avimelek continued speaking with Avraham, and said: "Why did you do this?"

11   Avraham answered, "Because I thought that there was no fear of God in this place, so that I would be killed on my wife's account.

12   And actually she is my sister—she is the daughter of my father. But she's not my mother's daughter, so she became my wife.

13 Then when God brought me out of my father's house, I told her to do me a loving favor and tell everyone wherever we go that, 'He is my brother.'"

14 So Avimelek took sheep, cattle, and male and female servants, and gave them to Avraham. He also gave his (Avraham's) wife Sarah back to him.

15 Afterward, Avimelek said, "Here, my entire land lays before you; live wherever you would like!"

16 He also told Sarah, "Here, I have given one thousand pieces of silver to your brother. I do this in front of everyone in order to clear the air on everything between us. You are innocent of everything."

17 Then Avraham prayed to God, and God healed Avimelek and his wife, as well as the court women of childbearing age. Only then could they give birth.

18 This is because God had made every woman in Avimelek's royal house absolutely infertile because of what happened concerning Sarah, the wife of Avraham.

Chapter 21

1   Afterward, God visited Sarah, just as He had said, and did exactly what He said He would do.

2   So Sarah became pregnant and bore a son to Avraham, even though he was old, at exactly the time that God had indicated.

3   Avraham named his son that Sarah had borne to him Isaac.

4   Then Avraham circumcised his son Isaac when he was eight days old, just as God commanded him.

5   And Avraham was one hundred years old when his son Isaac was born to him.

6   Sarah said, "God has given me a great reason to laugh in joy. Everyone who hears about this will laugh with me."[1]

7   So she said, "Who could have told Avraham that I would be nursing children? But I have born him a son in his old age!"

8   And the child grew and was weaned. So Avraham held a festive meal on the day of Isaac's weaning.

9   Sarah saw the son of Hagar, the Egyptian who bore Avraham a son, as he was making fun of (Isaac).

10 So she said to Avraham, "Throw out this concubine and her son, because the son of this concubine will not share in the inheritance of Isaac, my son."

11 Avraham was deeply grieved by this action concerning his son.

12 Then God spoke with Avraham, "Don't be grieved about the youth and about your concubine. Listen to everything that Sarah has said to you, because your inheriting lineage will come through Isaac.

13 And I will also make the son of the concubine into a nation, since he is your descendant."

---

1. Isaac means "laughter" in Hebrew. See note 3 to chapter 17.

14 So Avraham got up early in the morning, took some bread and a skin of water, and gave it to Hagar, putting it on her shoulders. Then along with the boy, he sent her away into the wilderness by Beersheva.

15 When all of the water in the skin was gone, she put the boy under a bush.

16 She then walked away and sat down about a bowshot away, because she said, "I cannot stand to see the boy die." So she sat down, and then she broke down and cried.

17 And God heard the cry of the boy. A messenger angel called out to Hagar from the heavens, saying to her, "What is the matter, Hagar? Don't fear, because God has heard the boy's cry all the while that he's been here.

18 Get up, take the boy and hold his hand, as I will make him a great nation."

19 Then God opened up her eyes and she saw a well. She went and filled the water skin with well water and gave a drink to the boy.

20 As time went on, God was with the boy, and he grew up living in the desert. He became a skilled bowman.

21 He settled in the desert area of Paran, and his mother found an Egyptian woman for him to marry.

22 During this time, Avimelek and his military commander Picol told Avraham, "God is with you in everything that you do.

23 So swear an oath to me in the name of God that because of the kindness with which I treated you, that you will not mistreat me or my grandchildren, or their descendants. Act this way toward me and all my kingdom."

24 Avraham replied, "I will swear such an oath."

25 Then Avraham complained to Avimelek about a well that Avimelek's servants had taken by force.

26 Avimelek answered, "I know nothing about who did this, and you didn't tell me right away. I haven't heard a thing about this until today."[2]

---

2. *v.* 26: It is possible that Avimelek here refers to the fact that Avraham did not tell

27 So Avraham took sheep and cattle, and gave them to Avimelek, by which the two of them made a covenant between them.

28 Avraham designated seven female lambs to be taken away by themselves.

29 Avimelek said to Avraham, "What are these seven lambs that are here, standing off by themselves?"

30 Then he replied, "Take these seven lambs from me to witness to the fact that I dug this well."

31 Therefore the name of this place was called Beersheva, because both of them swore an oath there.[3]

32 So they made an oath at Beersheva, after which Avimelek and his military commander Picol got up and returned to the land of the Philistines.

33 Then he (Avraham) planted a tamarisk tree in Beersheva, and there he called on the name of God, the Everlasting God.

34 Afterward, Avraham lived in the land of the Philistines for a long time.

---

him the name of the person(s) who took the well until he complained, as opposed to the timing of the complaint. Both understandings are possible, given the text. I have translated the verse to be referring to the timing of the complaint.

3. The name "Beersheva" has a double meaning: *be'er* is a well, and *sheva* can mean either "oath" or "seven." Thus, the name can mean "well of the oath" or "seven wells," perhaps "seventh well."

Chapter 22

The Akeida (Binding of Isaac)

1 It was after these events that God made Avraham pass through a great ordeal. So He said to him, "Avraham." He (Avraham) replied, "I'm right here!"[1]

2 He told him, "Please take your only son that you love, Isaac; then hurry to the Land of Moriah. While there, climb up one of the hills that I will designate to you."

3 So Avraham got up early in the morning, and saddled his donkey. He took two youths with him, along with Isaac his son. As well, he bundled wood together for a whole burnt offering. Then he left to go to the place that God told him about.

4 On the third day, Avraham looked and saw this place from a distance.

5 Avraham said to his youths, "Stay here with the donkey, and the boy and I will go and prostrate ourselves in worship. Then we'll return to you."

6 So Avraham took the wood for the whole burnt offering and put them on Isaac his son (to carry). Then he took the kindling wood and the slaughtering knife by hand, and the two of them went off together.

1. *v.* 1: The Hebrew word *akeida* means "binding," and this is the central event of this chapter—the great trial that happened to Avraham through the binding of his son Isaac. Jewish writings see this event as extremely important in the history of the three Patriarchs and thus of the historical nation of Israel. In fact, on the Jewish holy day of Rosh HaShanah (the calendral new year), rams' horns are blown in every Jewish community as part of the holy day's ceremony (cf. Leviticus 23. 24–25). The Talmud records: "Rabbi Abbahu taught, 'Why is the shofar (the ram's horn) blown (on Rosh HaShanah)?' The Holy One commanded, '"Blow the ram's horn before Me, in order that I will recall the binding (*akeidah*) of Isaac the son of Avraham"' (Rosh HaShanah 16a). Thus it was Jewish tradition from the times of Rabbi Abahu (early fourth century AD) that the *akeidah* gave even more meaning to the rituals of Rosh HaShanah. For more on the significance of the *akeidah*, I refer the reader to the excellent background article, "The Eternal Akeidah" by Rabbi Nosson Scherman, found in *"Tashlich"*, Mesorah Publications, 2006.

7 It was then that Isaac spoke to Avraham his father, saying, "My father," to which he replied, "I am already here, my son." So he continued, "Here is the kindling and the wood, but where is the lamb for the whole burnt offering?"

8 Avraham answered, "God Himself will provide the lamb for the whole burnt offering, my son." And the two of them continued to walk together.

9 Then they came to the place that God had told him about. Avraham built an altar there and arranged the wood. He also tied up his son Isaac and put him on the altar, above the wood.

10 Avraham reached up and took the slaughtering knife, with which to slaughter his son.

11 Suddenly a messenger angel of God called out to him from Heaven, saying: "Avraham! Avraham!" So he answered, "I'm right here!"

12 He continued, "Don't lift a finger against the boy! Don't do anything to him, because now I know that you truly fear God! You did not keep your son, your only son, back from me."[2]

13 Avraham looked into the distance, and he saw that a ram was caught in a bush by its horns. So Avraham went there and took the ram and offered it up as a whole burnt offering instead of his son.

14 So Avraham called the name of that place "Adonay yir'aeh," which is to say that "today at this hill, God was seen."[3]

2. *v.* 12: An overall question that is in the background of the *akeida* is whether God really intended for Avraham to physically sacrifice his son. The extant opinion on that question is "no," as reflected in this Talmudic opinion: ". . . (the phrase) 'I (God) had not commanded' refers to the sacrifice of the son of Mesha the King of Moab by his father (2 Kings, 3.27): 'now spoken' refers to the daughter of Jephthah; and 'which had not come into my mind' refers to Isaac, whom his father Abraham was willing to sacrifice" (Ta'anit 4a). That is, we are taught here that God did not wish Isaac to die. The willingness of Avraham to fully obey God was the issue at stake. The three situations mentioned here, that of King Mesha's son, that of the judge Jephthah's daughter, and that of Isaac, involved the issue of parents and the possible death of their children by the parents' own hands. God is portrayed as not wanting the death of the children by the parents in all three of these situations.

3. *v.* 14: The Hebrew word *yir'aeh* can have a number of possible understandings. It can mean "seen" (CJB translation, and mine here); it can also refer to God being "feared" (though the Masoretic text may argue against this understanding of such a meaning), or

15 Then a messenger angel of God again called out to Avraham from Heaven,

16 and said, "'Indeed, I swear by Myself,' says God, 'that truly because you did this action and did not keep back your only son,

17 I will greatly bless you and greatly increase your descendants (in number) as the stars of the sky and like the sand on the seashore. Your descendants will inherit the city gates of their enemies.

18 And all nations on earth will have reason to bow their knees in thanksgiving because of your descendants, because you listened to and obeyed My voice.'"

19 So Avraham returned to his two youths, and they all got up and left together for Beersheva. Then Avraham lived in Beersheva.

20 After these events, Avraham was told, "Milkah also gave birth to children for your brother Nachor's clan:

21 Utz, his firstborn; Buz, his brother, and Kemu'el, the patriarch of Aram;

22 Kesed, Chazo, Pildash, Yidlaf, and Betu'el."

23 Then Betu'el fathered Rivkah. These eight (sons) were borne by Milkah to Nachor, the brother of Avraham.

24 He (Nachor) had a concubine named Re'umah, and she also gave birth to Tevach, Gacham, Tachash, and Ma'acah.

"worshipped" (Targum), as well as "revealed" (Targum Neofiti). Thus, one's contextual understanding of the flow of the text could determine one's translation of this word. *v.* 18: The Hebrew word *shema* refers not only to the physical act of hearing but the follow-up actions that are inherently connected to the message that is heard (cf. Deut. 6.4ff). Thus I have rendered *shema* as "listened to and obeyed".

Chapter 23

1 Sarah lived to be 127 years old.

2 And so Sarah died at Kiryat Arba, that is, Hevron, in the land of Canaan. Avraham mourned for Sarah and wept over her loss.

3 Avraham left the place where Sarah had died and spoke to the Hittites, saying,

4 "I am a foreigner, and a temporary resident in your midst. Grant me land for burial, so I can bury my dead."

5 The Hittites answered Avraham, saying to him,

6 "We have heard your request, sir. You are like a high official from God in our midst. So take our choice burial ground, and bury your dead in a tomb. None of us will refuse to let you bury your dead in his tomb."

7 Then Avraham went to the Hittites and prostrated himself before them, the holders of the land.[1]

8 And he spoke with them, saying, "If there is any one of you who will let me bury my dead (on his land), let it be Efron ben Sohar. Talk to him and request this on my behalf:

9 that he grant me the cave at Machpelah, which is at the edge of his field. I will buy it for full price, so that I may have a burial site in your territory."

10 Efron was sitting with the Hittite elders. So Efron the Hittite answered Avraham publicly, in front of all who were present at the town gate, saying,[2]

---

1. *vv.* 7 *and* 12: Avraham bows to them as a sign of respect, not in idolatrous worship.

2. *v.* 10: This is the place where much business, including legal transactions, were carried out in the ancient world. This verse has a possible alternative meaning: Efron may not have physically sat in the town's gate but possibly is being described as being a resident of Hittite society (with choice land that then Avraham requests to buy). The Hebrew word used, *yoshev*, can have that nuance. However, I favor the translation that I used, where he is depicted as sitting in the business area of his town. Here he and Avraham could carry out this legal transaction together in front of Hittite witnesses. It appears in

11 "No, sir, listen to me. . . . I will give you the field with the burial cave in it. I give it to you, as witnessed by my people. It is given to you, so go and bury your dead."

12 Then Avraham prostrated himself before the Hittites.

13 And he spoke to Efron before the witnesses, saying, "Please, just listen to me—I want to buy the field with money. Take it from me, and then I will bury my dead there."

14 So Efron answered Avraham and said to him,

15 "Sir, now listen to me; 400 shekels of silver for the land is not a high sum between you and me. It's nothing. Now go and bury your dead."

16 Avraham did what Efron suggested and weighed that sum of money that was agreed upon in front of the Hittite elders: 400 shekels of silver to complete this legal business transaction.

17 Included in this transaction were the field of Efron that included Machpelah, close to Mamre; the field, the burial cave that was in it, and every tree that was in the field or bordering around it.

18 This was Avraham's purchase, witnessed to by the Hittites and all who were by the town gate.

19 After this event, Avraham buried Sarah, his wife, in the cave in the field of Machpelah, by Mamre, which is Hevron, in the land of Canaan.

20 So the field and the cave that is in the field became Avraham's legal property, to be a burial place, (bought) from the Hittites.[3]

---

v. 11 that Efron is answering the specific request of Avraham from v. 9 to purchase the field ("no sir, listen to me. . . . I will give you the field . . ."). He may have been summoned there by his elders to carry out the described transaction.

3. v. 20: The Hebrew word vayaqam in my translation shows legal force; thus in v. 17 and here in v. 20, vayaqam should be seen as a result of the legal transaction that occurred.

Chapter 24

1 So Avraham was old; he had become elderly. God had blessed Avraham in every area of life.

2 Then Avraham spoke to his senior servant, who was in charge of his affairs: "Please put your hand under my thigh.[1]

3 I am putting you under an oath, by the Lord God of the Heavens and the God of the earth, that you will not take a wife for my son from the Canaanite women, in whose midst I live.

4 Instead, you will go to my land, to my homeland, and there you will take a wife for my son Isaac."

5 So the servant said to him, "Maybe the young lady will refuse to return here with me. If so, should I return there with your son, to the land of your origin?"

6 Avraham replied to him, "Be careful never to bring my son there.

7 The Lord God of Heaven Who brought me from my father's house and from the land of my birth, and Who spoke to me, swearing to me, saying, 'To your descendants I will give this Land,' it is He who will send his messenger angel before you so that you will find a wife for my son Isaac.

8 And if the young lady refuses to go with you, you are then free from this oath to me. I only ask that my son not go there."

9 So the servant put his hand under his clan chief Avraham's thigh, and swore an oath to him concerning this very matter.

10 The servant then took ten camels from his clan chief, and he left with his best supplies. He left for Aram Naharayim, for the town of Nachor.

---

1. 1v. 2: This was an ancient Middle Eastern gesture akin to swearing an oath (similar perhaps to the modern placing of one's right hand on holy writ before testifying in a court.)

11   After this, he rested the camels on their knees outside of the town, at the well. It was evening, the time for drawing water.

12   Then he said, "Lord God of my clan chief Avraham, please show me kindness today by taking pity on my clan chief Avraham.

13   Here I am, standing at the water spring, and young women who live in the town are coming out to draw water.

14   May it be that the young lady to whom I say, 'Please give me a drink from your water jug,' and who tells me, 'Drink, and I will also give water to your camels,' that she be fit for Your servant Isaac. Then I will know that You have shown covenant-based love to my clan chief."

15   Before he even stopped praying, Rivkah appeared with her water jug on her shoulders. She was the daughter of Betu'el, the son of Milkah, the wife of Nachor, Avraham's brother.

16   This young lady was absolutely stunning. She was unmarried; she descended down to the spring, and filled her jug, then came back up.

17   So the servant ran to meet her, and said, "Please let me have a little water from your jug."

18   Then she replied, "Drink, sir," as she hurriedly lowered her water jug into her hands, and then gave him some water.

19   When she finished giving him water, she said, "I can also give your camels water until they stop drinking."

20   So she quickly poured out her jug into the drinking trough and ran again to the well to draw water to give to his camels.

21   The man was astonished by her, and he wanted to know if God was helping him and giving him this success, or not.

22   When the camels finished drinking, the man took a gold nose-ring that had silver fillings, and two bracelets for her hands. They weighed ten shekels in gold.

23   So he said, "Young lady, just who are you? Please tell me. Is there any chance that there is room for us to stay overnight at your father's home?"

24 She responded to him, "I am the daughter of Betu'el the son of Milkah, who bore him for Nachor."

25 She continued, saying to him, "We have lots of straw and hay, and also a place to sleep."

26 Then the man bowed down and prostrated himself in worship to God.

27 He said, "Blessed is the Lord God of my clan chief, Avraham. He has not forgotten His covenant love and His faithfulness to him, for while traveling, I was brought by God to the relatives of the brother of my clan chief."

28 So the young lady ran and told her mother all that happened.

29 Rivkah had a brother named Lavan. He rushed off to see the man who was at the outskirts of the spring.

30 When he saw the nose-ring and the bracelets on the hands of his sister, and as he heard his sister Rivkah's explanation, that the man had said this-and-that to her, he went out to find the man. Sure enough, the man was with his camels, at the spring.

31 And he said, "Come! Blessed is God! Why are you standing outside? I have made room for you at home, and for your camels, as well."

32 So the man came to the home, where the camels were unloaded and given straw and hay. Water was given to wash his (Avraham's servant's) feet, as well as the feet of the men who came with him.

33 Then he was given food to eat, but he said, "I can't eat until I say what I need to say."

34 And he said, "I am Avraham's servant.

35 God has greatly blessed my clan chief and he has become an important man. He has given him sheep, cattle, silver and gold, male and female servants, camels and donkeys.

36 Sarah, the wife of my chief, has given birth to a son for him, well after he was elderly. He has given him all that he has!

37 So my chief has sworn me to an oath, saying, 'Do not take a wife for my son from among Canaanite women, in whose midst and territory I live.

38 Instead, go to my father's relatives, to my family there, and take a wife for my son.'"

39 So I said to my clan chief, "What if the young lady refuses to come with me?

40 He responded to me, 'God, before Whom I have lived righteously, will send his messenger angel with you to help you succeed. And you will succeed in taking a wife for my son from my family, from my father's relatives.

41 So you will be released from my oath if you go to my family and they don't give (a young girl) to you. You will then be freed from my oath.'

42 When I came to the spring today, I said, 'Lord God of my clan chief Avraham, please give me success on the trip that I am on.

43 As I stand at the spring of water, if a young girl comes to draw water, and I say to her, 'Please, give me a little water from your jug,'

44 and then she says to me, 'You can drink, and also I will draw water for your camels," then may she be the young lady who You have prepared for my chief's son.'

45 I barely stopped praying this when Rivkah walked by with her jug on her shoulder, and she came down to the spring to draw water. So I said to her, 'Please give me water to drink.'

46 She hurried and lowered her jug and said, 'Drink, and I will also get water for your camels.' And so I drank, and so did the camels.

47 Then I asked her, 'Whose daughter are you?' So she told me that she was the daughter of Betu'el, the son of Nachor whose mother was Milkah. I then put the nose-ring on her nose and gave her the bracelets.[2]

48 Afterwards, I bowed down and fell prostrate in worship to God. I thanked the Lord God of my chief Avraham, Who led me on the true path by providing the niece of my chief (as a wife) for his son (Isaac).

2. *v.* 47: Actually, Rivkah was the granddaughter of Avraham's brother Nachor (cf. 22:20–23).

49 And now, if you will act with covenant love and in truth for my chief, tell me so. And if not, tell me, so that I will leave you alone. I'll make my way in any direction (out of your home)."[3]

50 So Lavan and Betu'el answered and said, "God is behind all of these events, so it's not our place to say yes or no.

51 Look, Rivkah is right here. Take her so she can be the wife of your chief's son, just as God told you."

52 When Avraham's servant heard these words, he prostrated himself in worship to God.

53 So the servant brought vessels of silver and gold along with garments and gave them to Rivkah. He then gave fine foods and delicacies to her brother and to her mother.

54 He and the men who had come with him ate and drank together. They slept there, and in the morning they rose up, and he (Avraham's servant) said, "Send me off to my chief with your blessings."

55 But her brother and mother said, "The girl will stay with us for a few days longer, maybe up to ten days, and then you can be on your way."

56 So he replied, "Please don't delay me; God will prosper my way. Send me off, so I can go to my chief."

57 Then they said, "We'll call for the girl, and we'll ask her ourselves (what she'd like to do)."

58 So they called for Rivkah, and said to her, "Do you want to go away with this man?" She said, "Yes, I want to go!"

59 As a result, her brother sent Rivkah off with Avraham's servants and with his men. She took her possessions, too.

60 They wished Rivkah well, saying to her, "Our sister, may you grow to be thousands upon ten thousands, and may your descendants inherit the gate of those who hate them."

61 So Rivkah and her attendants got up onto their camels and went with the man. The servant took Rivkah (with him), and off they went.

---

3. *v.* 49: In saying this, he signifies his willingness to immediately leave and "get out of Betu'el and Lavan's hair" if they don't like his proposal of marriage on Isaac's behalf.

62 Isaac came to the road to Beer-lachay-ro'i, and lived in the Negev desert region. So, Isaac went out to the fields around dusk in order to relax. He looked in the distance and saw that a caravan was coming.[4]

63 At the same time, Rivkah looked in the distance and saw Isaac.

64 She proceeded to fall off of her camel![5]

65 She asked the servant, "Who is this man who has come out to the field to meet us?" The servant answered, "He is my chief." So she covered her face with a veil.[6]

66 The servant described all the events that happened to Isaac.

67 So Isaac brought her into the tent of his mother, Sarah. He took Rivkah to be his wife, and he truly loved her. She comforted him after (the death of his mother).

4. v. 62: This name means "well of the living shepherd" or "well that gives life to shepherds" (logically, a well in the Negev Desert would do such).

5. v. 64: Here I interpret the text to be saying that Rivkah, taken up in the moment, lost her concentration and fell off her camel, as opposed to stopping her camel and dis¬mounting. The view that Rivkah was overwhelmed by the moment is an understanding that the great scholar and commentator Rashi favored (see glossary).

6. v. 65: The servant describes Isaac as his "chief," though technically Avraham was his ultimate clan chief, and the servant usually referred to him as such (cf. ch. 24: 48, 51, 54, 56).

Chapter 25

1   Then Avraham married another wife. Her name was Keturah.

2   She bore him Zimran, Yokshan, Midan, Midyan, Yishbak, and Shuach.

3   Yokshan's descendants were Sheva and Dedan. Dedan's descendants became Ashurim, Latushim, and other nationalities.

4   Midian's descendatns were Efah and Efer, Chanoch and Avida, and Elda'ah. These were all the sons of Keturah.

5   As well, Avraham gave presents to the sons of his concubines.

6   However, he sent them away from Isaac while they were all still living east of the land of Kedem.

7   Avraham's entire lifespan was 175 years.

8   And then Avraham passed away. He died at a very elderly age, stately and dignified to the very end. His clan then buried him.

9   His sons Isaac and Ishmael buried him in the cave of Machpelah, in the field of Efron ben Sohar the Hittite, which was by Mamre.

10   This was the field that Avraham bought from the Hittites. Both Avraham and Sarah his wife were buried there.

11   After Avraham died, God blessed Isaac his son. Isaac lived at Beer-lachay-ro'i (the Well of life for a shepherd).

12   This is the family history of Ishmael, Avraham's son, whom Sarah's servant Hagar the Egyptian bore for Avraham.

13   Ishmael's sons were named as follows: Nevayt, the first-born, then Kedar, Adbe'el, and Mevsam, respectively.

14   Then, Mishma, Dumah, and Masa;

15   Chadad, Tema, Yetur, Nafish, and Kedmah.

16   These were Ishmael's sons and their given names. They made up twelve rulers of different nations, each with a fortress in their given locations.

17 Ishmael lived to be 137 years old, and he passed away and died, and was buried by his clan.

18 They lived from Havilah to Shur, which borders Egypt from the road to Ashur. He died in the presence of his entire clan.

19 This is the family history of Isaac, Avraham's son. Avraham fathered Isaac.

20 Isaac was forty years old when he married Rivkah, Betu'el's daughter, the Aramite from Padan Aram, the sister of Lavan the Aramite.

21 And Isaac pleaded to God on behalf of his wife, because she was childless. Then God answered him, and Rivkah his wife became pregnant.

22 Her unborn boys were moving inside of her very actively, so she said, "I don't understand why this is happening to me," and she asked God why this was so.

23 So God said to her, "Two peoples are in your womb, two nations will emerge from inside of you, and be separated from each other. The stronger one will serve the younger one."

24 Her time to give birth came, and twins were in her womb.

25 The firstborn was born, and he was ruddy with hair all over his body. They named him Esav.

26 Afterwards, his brother was born, with his hand holding the heel of Esav. They named him Yakov. So Isaac was sixty years old when he fathered them.[1]

27 The boys grew up, and Esav became a skilled hunter, an outdoorsman, while Yakov became concerned with spiritual affairs and spent his time indoors.[2]

---

1. *v.* 26: The name Yakov literally means "the one at the heel," or "the one who follows," and describes his birth order and appearance at birth. His name, contrary to popular belief, does not mean "supplanter" or "deceiver," in any way whatsoever.

2. *v.* 27: the Hebrew word *tam* is not easy to translate in this context. I prefer a translation and meaning where Yakov is set in juxtaposition to Esav, as in "one concerned with spiritual affairs." One son (Esav) is concerned with obtaining food; the other son is concerned with more eternal and ethereal matters. I believe the inference of the Hebrew text points us in that direction. Levin translates this word as "righteous" or "complete" (perhaps a more "well-rounded" person, due to his interest in spiritual affairs). Levin's translation is also possible (see Y. Levin, "The Meaning of TMM in Gen. 25:27," e-mail

28 Isaac showed favoritism to Esav, because his hunting skills put food on his table. Rivkah, though, showed favoritism to Yakov.

29 Once, Yakov cooked a stew when Esav came in from the outdoors, thoroughly exhausted.

30 So Esav said to Yakov, "Give me a little of that red-colored stew, because I'm really exhausted." Because of this, his name was called Edom.³

31 Yakov replied, "Sell me your firstborn inheritance rights today."

32 Then Esav said, "Look, I'm going to die, so what good to me (are my rights) as the firstborn?"

33 So Yakov stated, "Swear an oath to me today." And Esav made an oath to him and sold his rights as the firstborn son.

34 Yakov had already given Esav bread and lentil stew, which he ate and drank. He then got up and left. So Esav did not consider his legal rights as the firstborn to be of any value.⁴

---

to b-hebrew mailing list, July 12, 2007, http://lists.ibiblio.org/ pipermail/b-hebrew/2007 July/032880.html).

3. *v.* 30: That is, Esav's descendants were called the Edomites (in Hebrew, literally "red people,"), because their patriarch uttered these words during this incident. In a similar linguistic vein, the first man in chapters 1 and 2 is referred to as *adam* in Hebrew, meaning "reddish," perhaps "earth colored," or attesting to his origins (i.e. "made from the earth," cf. 2.7).

4. *v.* 34: An interesting interpretation of this section is offered by Rabbi Hillel Goldberg: ". . . How could Jacob withhold food from Esau as he comes back from the field famished? Esau says he will die of hunger, so he sells his birthright to Jacob. Where is the ethics in Jacob's wresting the birthright by holding over Esau the threat of hunger? The biblical text seem to make it perfectly clear that this is just what Jacob does.... Translations err when they write, "And Jacob gave Esau bread .. ." The Hebrew seems to read, *And Jacob gave bread;* subject, verb, object. However, Biblical Hebrew has no way of expressing the past participle other than word order. "He had given" cannot be said in Hebrew, only "he gave." How, then, does Hebrew indicate, "He had given"? By a subtle change in word order. When the Hebrew wants to indicate the past *tense*, it writes the verb before the subject, literally "and gave Jacob" (*va-yiten* Ya'akov). But when it wants to indicate the past participle, its word order is literally "and Jacob gave" (*ve-Ya'akov natan*), meaning "and Jacob *had* given." Meaning, in our context: "and Jacob had already given Esau bread and lentil stew" when they were negotiating over the birthright. Jacob was not holding food over Esau's head, coercing him to surrender his birthright." In my translation, I have followed Goldberg's interpretation from his article, "Does Order in the Torah Make a Difference?" *Jewish World Review*, November 28, 2003, http://www .jewishworldreview.com/hillel/goldberg_2003_11_28 (accessed June 23, 2009).

Chapter 26

1   There was a famine in the Land, in addition to the first famine that occurred in the time of Avraham. So Isaac went to Avimelek, the king of the Philistines in Gerar.

2   God appeared to him and said, "Don't go down into Egypt; live in the Land that I will tell you about.

3   Live in this Land, and I will be with you. I will give you reasons to bow your knees in thanksgiving, because I will give all of these territories to you and your descendants. I will bring to pass the entire oath that I swore to Avraham your father.

4   And I will make your descendants as numerous as the stars in the sky. I will give your descendants all these territories. All peoples of the world will have reason to bow their knees in thanksgiving because of your descendants.

5   This is because Avraham heard and obeyed My voice, and he kept My commandments, as well as My teachings that are not based on logic; and he also (kept) My Torah."

6   So Isaac lived in Gerar.

7   The local inhabitants asked him about his wife, to which he responded, saying, "She's my sister". He did not say "my wife," out of fear that the locals would murder him because Rivkah was beautiful and very striking to look at.

8   After Isaac had been there for a while, Avimelek king of the Philistines glanced out of his window and saw that Isaac was caressing his wife Rivkah.[1]

---

1. *v.* 8: This verse leaves the impression that Isaac was confined to the king's quarters or palace until the king had decided what he would do with Rivkah. Perhaps such a confinement occurred between *v.* 7 and 8 in our text. Indeed, where was it that Isaac "had been"? (cf.*v.* 8). Perhaps in Gerar, but more probably confined to the king's quarters so he would not leave with his beautiful "sister" until the king decided what to do. It could be that one of the royal family members was infatuated with her (cf. v. 10, "one of our men").

9 So Avimelek summoned Isaac, and said, "Look, it's clear that she's your wife. Why did you say 'she's my sister?'" Then Isaac answered him, "I said this since I thought I would die because of her."

10 Then Avimelek said, "What have you done to us? One of my men could have had sexual relations with your wife and brought about legal guilt upon us all."

11 Avimelek issued an order to all of his people, stating, "Anyone who lays a hand on either this man or his wife will be summarily executed."

12 Isaac then sowed seeds in that land, which he reaped a hundred times over that same year. So God blessed him.

13 So he became wealthier and wealthier, and grew greatly in influence.

14 He had so many flocks of sheep, herds of cattle, and servants that the Philistines became envious of him.

15 All of the wells that his father Avraham's servants had dug during his lifetime had been plugged up by the Philistines, who then filled them with dirt.

16 Then Avimelek told Isaac, "Leave us. You have become much more powerful than we are."

17 So Isaac left there and pitched his tents at the wadi of Gerar, and he settled there.

18 While he lived there, Isaac redug water wells that were dug during his father Avraham's lifetime but had been plugged up by the Philistines after the death of Avraham. He then called them by the same names that his father had called them.

19 Isaac's servants dug by the wadi, and they found a fresh water well there.

20 Then the shepherds of Gerar got into a dispute with Isaac's shepherds. They claimed, "That's our water!" So he named the well "Exploitation," because they (the shepherds of Gerar) exploited him.

21 So they (Isaac's servants) dug an alternate well, but the shepherds disputed it, as well. So he (Isaac) named it "Opposition."

22 So he moved on from there, and dug another well, over which there was no dispute. He named it "Open Spaces." because "now God has given us 'elbow room', so we can prosper in the Land."

23 Then he went from there to Beersheva.

24 God appeared to him during that night, and said, "I am the God of Avraham your father; do not be afraid because I am with you and will give you reasons to bend your knees in thanksgiving. I will make your descendants numerous because of my servant Avraham."

25 So he erected an altar and called on the name of God. Pitching his tents there, the servants of Isaac also dug a well at that place.

26 Then Avimelek came to him from Gerar, accompanied by Ahuzat, his advisor, and by Picol, his military commander.

27 Isaac said to them, "Why have you come to me? None of you like me, and you already expelled me from your midst!"

28 So they replied, "We've certainly seen that God has been with you. We said to ourselves, 'There should be an agreement between all of us; between us and you; so let's make a covenant with you,

29 stipulating that you will not do anything evil toward us since we haven't harmed you, and we have done only good towards you.' We sent you away in peace, so now you are blessed by God."

30 He (Isaac) then prepared a covenant meal for them, and they ate and drank.

31 They woke up early in the morning, and everyone swore oaths to each other. Then Isaac sent them away from him in peace.

32 On that same day, Isaac's servants came and told him about the well that they dug. They told him, "We found water."

33 He called it (the well) "Oath." Because of this, the name of the city is called Beer- sheva till today.

34 Esav was forty years old when he married his wives, Yehudit bat Be'eri the Hittite and Basmat bat Elon, also a Hittite.[2]

---

2. *v. 34:* The Hebrew word *sheva* means either "oath" or "seven"; again we are told why Beersheva was given that name (cf. 21.31).

Chapter 27

1 Isaac was now elderly and had serious problems with his eyesight. He called his firstborn son Esav and said to him: "My son," and he answered back to him, "I'm here."

2 He (Isaac) said, "Look, I'm elderly now, and I don't know when I will die.

3 So now, please get your hunting gear, your quiver and your bow, then go out into the wild and hunt some game for me.

4 Then make me the tasty kinds of food that I like and bring them to me so that I can eat them. I'll then be able to give you blessings before I die."

5 Rivkah heard what Isaac said to Esav his son. So Esav went into the wild to hunt and bring back game.

6 Rikvah then spoke to Yakov her son, saying, "Look, I heard what your father said to Esav your brother:

7 'Bring me game, and make delicious food for me, so I can eat it. Then I'll pass on the blessings of God to you before my death.'

8 So now, my son, listen to me concerning what I am about to tell you.

9 Please go to the flock, and take two of the best young goats from there. Then I will make them into tasty foods, just the way that your father loves.

10 You'll bring it to your father, and he'll eat it, so that he will pass the blessings on to you before his death."

11 Yakov told Rivkah his mother, "But my brother Esav is very hairy, and I'm smooth skinned.

12 Maybe my father will touch or caress me, and then he'll think that I'm trying to trick him. Then he'll curse me and not pass on the blessing."[1]

---

1. *v.12:* The Hebrew wording here, *yemusheni*, is more than a simple touch. It also intimates a rubbing, or a tender caress. Being that Isaac was sight-impaired, perhaps he

13 His mother responded to him, "Then your curse will fall upon me, my son. But listen to me, and go and get for me (what I asked of you)."

14 So he went, took and brought (them) to his mother. Then his mother made the tasty foods, just like his father loved.

15 Then Rivkah took her elder son Esav's familiar clothes that were at home, and she dressed her youngest son Yakov in them:[2]

16 she put goatskins on his arms and on his smooth neck.

17 Then she gave the tasty foods, along with bread that she had baked, to her son Yakov.

18 So he went to his father and said, "My father." He responded: "Here I am. Which son are you?"

19 Yakov replied to his father, "I am Esav, your firstborn. I did exactly what you requested of me. Please sit up and eat my game, so that you can pass on the blessing to me."

20 Isaac then said to his son, "How did you find game so fast, my son?" He replied, "The Lord your God had everything prepared for me."

21 Then Isaac said to Yakov, "Come here, and let me stroke you, my son, so I may know whether or not you are my son Esav."

22 Yakov went over to Isaac his father, and he (Isaac) caressed him, saying, "Your voice is Yakov's voice, but you have the arms of Esav."

23 So he didn't recognize him because his arms were so similar to those of Esav his brother: hairy. Then he (Isaac) warmed up to him,

24. after which he said, "You are my son Esav, yes?" So he (Yakov) answered, "I am."

25 "Come over here to me, and let me eat the food from my son's hunting trip, so that I will be able to pass on the blessing to you." He brought

---

recognized people by his sense of touch, much as some sight-impaired persons today will feel the outline of someone's face to gain greater intimacy.

2. v.15: the Hebrew word connotes clothing that would have been familiar to Isaac; thus, they were garments that were typical of Esav's dress. "Typical" could have been the word used for "familiar" here, but I chose the latter, since the purpose would be to use clothes that were familiar to Isaac and characteristic of Esav. The next verse delineates what some of these clothes were.

(the food) to him, and he (Isaac) ate it. He (Yakov) also brought wine for him to drink.

26 Then Isaac, his father, said to him, "Come here, please, and kiss me, my son."

27 So he approached him and kissed him, and he (Isaac) smelled the scent of his clothes. Then Isaac blessed him, saying, "See, the smell of my son is like the smell of the outdoors, which God has blessed.[3]

28 May God give you dew from the Heavens, and abundant grain and wine from the fat of the Land.

29 May peoples serve you and nations bow down to you; may you be mightier than your brother; may the sons of your mother be subject to you. May those who curse you be cursed; and those who bless you be blessed!"[4]

3. *v. 27:* One rabbinic tradition is that this "smell of the outdoors" was a pleasant smell: "...and he (Isaac) said, 'Look, the scent of my son is like the smell of the outdoors that God has blessed. Rabbi Yehudah taught after the tradition of Rabbi Shmuel bar Shila . . . (Isaac meant) the smell of an apple orchard": Ta'anit 29b, http://www.e-daf.com/index.asp (accessed June 23, 2009); author's translation.

4. *v. 29:* This particular narrative brings up a matter of perspective. Many of my students throughout the years read the text portraying Yakov as a sneaky, conniving, no-good-for anything robber of his brother's blessings. That is not how I read the text. One must remember that God Himself showed Rivkah *while she was pregnant* which son was to be the prominent one who would inherit the blessings, including the passing on of the ancestral covenant blessings. I believe that our Torah portrays Esav as totally indifferent to matters concerning the covenants. As the Torah records: "So Esav despised his birthrights." Indeed, he had legally sold his rights to these blessings to Yakov earlier in the text. Apparently, Esav had never informed Isaac that this transaction had occurred! A greater deception was that Esav, who now had no rights to the blessings, was going to pretend that he deserved them anyway and that he was the rightful heir to the blessings. But Yakov had acquired them, and now under Rivkah's inspiration, he was fighting for what was his. He did so in the only manner in which he and his mother could, so that the precious covenants of God would carry on through Isaac's descendants. Yes, they lied to Isaac. But so did Esav try to deceive Isaac. This was a fierce, passionate battle for God's promises, in which the rightful son won. Let us remember the issue that was at stake. As Rabbi Shlomo Riskin noted in his commentary on this text, "Up for grabs is the destiny of the Jewish people—a nation chosen by God to bring the divine blessing to all the families of Earth . . . it is no less than the preservation and perpetuation of the Abrahamic mission and vision . . . Perpetuation also requires a steadfast continuation of the unique lifestyle, values and goals which Abraham taught: commitment to the one God, familial dedication, compassionate justice. The bearer of this gift may be said to have received the birthright (*bechora*)" ("Parashat Vayeshev: The Leaders and the Led," *Jerusalem Post*, December 18, 2008).

30 After Isaac had finished passing on the blessings to Yakov, and well after Yakov had left Isaac his father, Esav his brother arrived from his hunting venture.

31 He had also prepared tasty food, which he brought to his father. So he said to his father, "Please get up, my father, and eat from your son's hunt, so that you will be able to pass on the blessing to me."

32 So Isaac his father asked him, "Who are *you*?" "I am your son, your firstborn, Esav!"

33 Then Isaac trembled in very great fear. He said, "Then who is the hunter who brought me game before you came, and I ate from it, then blessed him? It is *he* who will be greatly blessed!"

34 When Esav heard the words of his father, he let out a very loud, bitter shout. Then he said to his father, "Pass on blessings to me, too, my father."

35 But he said, "Your brother came (to me) insincerely and took away your blessing."

36 So he (Esav) said, "Then he is as his name, Yakov, because now he has taken away my blessing twice. Once again, he has stolen my blessing! Can't you give me a blessing?"[5]

37 Isaac answered, saying to Esav, "Look, I've made him mightier than you, and all of his brother's descendants will be his servants; I have given him grain and wine. What's left for me to give you, my son?"

38 So Esav said to his father, "Don't you have just one blessing, my father; bless me also, my father." Then Esav began to weep.

---

5. *v.* 36: Esav's comment gives us the source for the erroneous belief that "Yakov" means "supplanter," "deceiver," or "trickster." He was making a snide comment about his brother. That was Esav's interpretation of how events unfolded between the two of them. Let us remember, though, how Esav is viewed in biblical literature. First we have the words of the prophet Malachi (1.3, author's translation): "I (God) hated Esav. . . ." And again in Hebrews (12.16): ". . no one (should be) sexually immoral, or Godless like Esav, who in exchange for a single meal gave up his rights as the firstborn (CJB)." This should throw a great amount of doubt on Esav's viewpoint here. *v.* 45: I assume that Rivkah here refers to both Isaac and Yakov, and not Esav and Yakov when she states "both of you."

39 Then Isaac his father answered, saying to him, "Here . . . may your residence be full of the fat of the Land, and of the dew from the Heavens above.

40 You will brandish your sword, yet serve your brother. But when you rebel, you will break his yoke off of your neck."

41 So Esav hated Yakov because of the blessings that he received from their father. Esav said to himself, "After the mourning period for my father is over, I am going to kill Yakov my brother."

42 Rivkah was told about her eldest son Esav's plans. So she sent for Yakov her younger son, and said to him, "Look, Esav your brother is going to try to console himself by killing you!

43 So now, my son, listen to me. Get up and flee to my brother Lavan in Haran!

44 Live with him for a while, till your brother's wrath ends.

45 When your brother's anger ends and he forgets what you did to him, then I'll send for you and bring you back from there. Why should I be bereaved of both of you on the same day?"

46 Then Rivkah said to Isaac, "If Yakov takes a Hittite woman, a woman from the people surrounding us as his wife, I will be devastated. My life will be worthless.

Chapter 28

1 Isaac called for Yakov, blessed him, then instructed him by saying to him, "Don't pick a wife from among the Canaanite women.

2 Get prepared to go to Padan-Aram, to the home of Betu'el, the father of your mother, and take a wife from among Lavan's daughters. He is your mother's brother.

3 And may Almighty God give you reason to bend your knee in worship; (may He) make you fruitful and numerous, that you may become a community of many people.

4 May He give the blessing of Avraham to both you and your descendants; may you inherit the Land where you live, (the Land) that God gave to Avraham."

5 Isaac then sent Yakov off to Padan-Aram, to Lavan the son of Betu'el the Aramite, brother of Rivkah, the mother of Yakov and Esav.

6 Then Esav found out that Isaac had blessed Yakov, and sent him off with a blessing to Padan-Aram to marry a wife from there; and he instructed him, saying, "Don't choose a Canaanite as a wife."

7 Yakov obeyed his father and mother, and went to Padan-Aram.

8 Esav then understood that his father Isaac despised Canaanite women.

9 So Esav went to Ishma'el and took Mahalat, the sister of Nevayot and the daughter of Ishma'el the son of Avraham, from among his women for the purpose of marriage.

10 Then Yakov left Beersheva and went to Haran.

11 When he came to an appropriate place, he spent the night there, since the sun had set. He took a rock from this place and put it under his head, then laid down in that same spot.[1]

---

1. *v.* 11: In the ancient Middle East, this served as a makeshift headrest, akin in function to the more modern pillow. In certain museums there, stone headrests of this sort are on display.

12 Then he had a dream in which there was a ladder standing on the ground with its top reaching high into the sky, with messenger angels of God going up and down on it.[2]

13 And there was God, standing on it. He said: "I am the Lord God of Avraham your father and the God of Isaac; the Land that you are laying on has been given by Me to you and to your descendants.

14 Your descendants will be like the dust on the ground; and you will expand toward the Mediterranean Sea, and eastward, and northwards, and toward the Negev desert. Every people on earth will have reason to bend their knee in thanksgiving to God because of you and your descendants.

15 Look, I am with you and will protect you everywhere you go. And I will bring you back to this Land, because I will not abandon you, even when I do everything that I have said to you."

16 Then Yakov woke up from his sleep, and said, "Wow! God is really present in this place, and I wasn't even conscious!"[3]

17 He became afraid and said, "How awesome this place is! This can be nothing but God's house, and the very gate to the Heavens."

18 When Yakov got up in the morning, he took the rock that he had put under his head, and put it up as a memorial marker. Then he poured oil on the top of it.

19 And he named this place "Bet-El"; the name of this town in former days had been Luz.

20 So Yakov made a vow, saying, "Because God will be standing with me and watches over me on this road that I travel on, and gives me bread to eat and clothes to wear,

---

2. *v.* 12: A nice insight is given into what this dream tells us about Yakov by Shlomo Riskin, the chief rabbi of Efrat, Israel. He wrote that ". . . it seems clear that the 'hands of Esau' (Jacob becoming the deceiver that Esau was) . . . is barely skin deep as far as Jacob's personality is concerned. Probably the greatest key to one's internal state of mind is one's dreams, and Jacob is surely dreaming of the Abrahamic mission: a ladder connecting heaven to earth, ascending and descending angels" ("Parashat Vayetze: In Goats' Clothing," *Jerusalem Post*, December 4, 2008).

3. *v.* 16: I believe that Yakov is referring to the fact that he was asleep (not "conscious") when he became aware of God's huge presence through the dream.

21 when I return in peace to my father's home, then God will be shown as my God.[4]

22 And this rock that I made into a marker will be "God's house," and from all that You give to me, I will give You back one-tenth of it."

---

4. *v.* 20-21: I realize that my translation flies in the face of traditional translations, which translate this verse to portray Yakov as making a conditional "deal" with God. However, this does not, in my opinion, fit the logical context or flow of the text. The Hebrew word *im* can certainly mean "if", as in "if God stands by me," However, Yakov had already been assured that God *would* be with him. In 35.3, he states his understanding of this very thing. So, I see this verse as a vow made out of gratefulness in reaction to God's promises to protect Yakov and to provide marvelously for his descendants (cf. v. 15). So, "God will be known as my God" (v. 21) because everyone would know that He brought Yakov back and provided for him, just as He promised. His faithfulness would be known to all. I do not view this as an "if you scratch my back, I'll scratch yours" deal, as if one could do such a thing with Almighty God! Instead, it is a faithful response to the great promises of the Holy One of Israel, akin to the type of 'vow' that Joseph is recorded as making in Bereshit 50.25. Let us remember that *Esav was considered an evil man*. ("I loved you", says God, "but you ask, 'how have You loved us?' Wasn't Esav the brother of Yakov? . . . I loved Yakov. But *I hated Esav*, and made his mountains a total ruin, and his inheritance I gave to the jackals of the wilderness." Malachi 1.2-3; author's translation and emphasis). Rivkah and Yakov understood Esav's makeup and acted aggressively to insure that the covenants would not be inherited by Esav. It is here that I wish to thank Dr. John Fischer, my mentor and teacher, for encouraging the development of this line of interpreting this text.

Chapter 29

1   Yakov then went with resolve toward the land of the eastern peoples.

2   He looked and saw a well in a field, where three flocks of sheep were lying down. Usually, the sheep would drink from it, but a big boulder was on top of the well opening.

3   All the flocks would be taken there, and the boulder was rolled off of the well opening. Then the flocks would drink, after which the boulder was returned to is place at the well opening.

4   So Yakov said to them, "Friends, where are you from?" They answered, "We are from Haran."

5   He then spoke to them, saying, "Do you know Lavan ben Nachor?" And they said, "We know him".[1]

6   "Is he well?" he asked. They responded, "(Yes, he's) well. Look, Rachel his daughter is coming with (his) sheep."

7   Then he said, "It's still daylight, so it's not time to gather the animals. Let the sheep drink, then go back to pasture."

8   So they said, "We can't until all the flocks are together and the stone is rolled off the well opening. Only then can we give water to the sheep."

9   He was still talking with them when Rachel came with her father's flock, since she knew how to shepherd.

10 When Yakov first saw Rachel, the daughter of Lavan his uncle, with her father's flock, he went and rolled the boulder off the well opening. He then watered the flock of Lavan, his uncle.[2]

---

1. *v.* 5: Lavan technically was 'ben Betu'el,' that is, the son of Bethu'el. However, as Nachor, the brother of Avraham, was the clan's founding chieftain, Lavan was known as "ben Nachor" (literally, the "son of Nachor"). This appellation may be a sign of respect to Nachor. However, it is possible that in this verse, the Hebrew word *ben* could mean "grandson" or simply "descendant."

2. *v.* 10–11: The verbs used in these verses use similar letters and have similar sounds, but the words have two different meanings. This means that there is a poetic pun-word-play between the words "to water" (*va-yashq*) in *v.* 10, and "to kiss" (*va-yishaq*) in *v.* 11.

11 And Jacob kissed Rachel and then in a loud voice began to weep.

12 Then Jacob told Rachel that he was a relative of her father, the son of Rivkah. So she ran to tell this to her father.

13 When Lavan heard the news about Jacob his nephew, he quickly ran to meet him. He hugged and kissed him, and brought him to his home. There, he (Yakov) explained everything to Lavan.

14 So Lavan said to him, "So, you are my kin and close relative!" He (Yakov) stayed with him for one month.

15 Then Lavan said to Yakov, "Even if you're my relative, should you work for me for nothing? Name your salary!"

16 Now Lavan had two daughters. The eldest was named Leah, and the younger was Rachel.

17 Leah had beautiful eyes, but Rachel was stunning in her beautiful appearance.[3]

18 Jacob had fallen in love with Rachel. So he said, "I will work for you for seven years for your younger daughter Rachel's hand."

19 So Lavan replied, "It's best for me to give her to you than to give her to any other man. So stay here and live with me."

20 And Jacob worked for Rachel seven years. It seemed to him like just a few days because of his great love for her.

21 Then Jacob said to Lavan, "It's time for me to marry and live with my wife, since I've put in my time."

22 Then Lavan gathered all the area's residents and made a wedding feast.

23 It was nightfall, and he (Lavan) took his daughter Leah and brought her to him (Yakov), and he had sexual relations with her.

3. v. 17: The Hebrew word *rakot* may mean "beautiful" (that is, her eyes; following the Targum), or may mean "diseased" (her eyes; following most other translations). We do not know which meaning is the correct one here. Either the comparison between the sisters is telling us that Leah had one beautiful feature, her eyes; but that her sister was more beautiful overall; or, the text may be telling us that Leah had an eye disease, which made her less attractive, while Rachel was quite attractive. Some have surmised that Leah was myopic (near-sighted) or had a watery, tearing eye disease, which is still a problem among some Arab populations today.

24 Lavan also gave his female servant Zilpah to his daughter Leah as her domestic servant.

25 When morning came, (Yakov realized) that (he was with) Leah. So he told Lavan, "What have you done to me? Didn't I work for you for Rachel? Why did you trick me?"

26 So Lavan replied, "It's not acceptable for us to give our younger daughter away before the oldest daughter.

27 Finish the bridal week, and I'll give you also (Rachel); then you'll work for me another seven years."[4]

28 Indeed, this is what Jacob did; he completed the bridal week, and then he (Lavan) gave him his daughter Rachel as a wife.

29 Lavan also gave his female servant Bilha to Rachel as her domestic servant.

30 He (Jacob) also had sexual relations with Rachel, whom he loved passionately and for whom he would work an extra seven years.

31 But God saw that Leah was shunned, so He made her fertile, while Rachel was childless.

32 And Leah became pregnant, giving birth to a son, whom she named Reuven. This is because she said, "God saw my painful troubles; but now my husband will love me."[5]

33 She became pregnant again and gave birth to another son, "Because God heard that I was shunned, so He gave me yet another (son)." She named him Shimon.[6]

---

4. *v.* 27: "Finishing the bridal week" would include participation in all of the wedding celebrations and meals, as well as taking part in the corporate joy. In other words, he would have to continue in this marriage to Leah. An interesting interpretation of this event, and of Yakov's entire time with Laban, is offered in the article "Good as His Word, Jacob Manipulates Justice" by Raymond Westbrook, *Biblical Archaeology Review* 35, no. 3 (2009): 50–55, 64, May/June 2009. I refer the reader to it, though this author does not fully agree with Westbrook's assessment of Yakov's behavior.

5. *v.* 32: "Reuven" in Hebrew means "He saw a son", referring to the fact that Leah suffered from lack of spousal love, but God showed her favor by granting her a son

6. *v.* 33: "Shimon" in Hebrew is connected to the word for "hear."

34 Then she became pregnant yet again, and gave birth to a son, saying, "Now, because of this, my husband will be with me, because I have borne him three boys." So she named him Levi.[7]

35 Once again she became pregnant and had a son, saying, "Now I thank God because (of this)," and she named him Yehudah. Then she stopped having children.[8]

---

7. *v.* 34: "Levi" in Hebrew is a derivative of the verb *lelavot*, meaning to accompany, or as translated here, "to be with."

8. v. 35: "Yehudah" means "one who gives thanks."

Chapter 30

1   Rachel realized that she had not given children to Yakov, and this made her jealous of her sister. She said to Yakov, "If you don't give me sons, I will die."

2   Then Yakov became angry at Rachel, and said, "Am I second to God? It is He Who decides if you will be fruitful!"

3   So she said, "Look, have sexual relations with my domestic servant, Bilha. I will (be the mother to) whom she bears, and I will start your family through her."

4   She gave him Bilha, her domestic servant, (to function as) a wife. And Yakov had sexual relations with her.

5   Then Bilha became pregnant and bore a son to Jacob.

6   Rachel then said, "God has judged my cause and heard my plea. So He gave me a son." Because of this, she named him Dan.[1]

7   Bilha, Rachel's domestic servant, became pregnant again and gave birth to a second son for Yakov.

8   Rachel said, "I fought intensely with my sister, and I won!" So she named him Naftali.[2]

9   Leah knew that she had stopped bearing children. So she took her domestic servant Zilpa and gave her to Yakov to (function as) a wife.

10 So Leah's domestic servant Zilpa bore Yakov a son.

11 Then Leah said, "Am I lucky!" So she named him Gad.[3]

12 And Leah's domestic servant Zilpa became pregnant and bore a second son to Yakov.

---

1. *v.* 6: "Dan" in Hebrew means "He has judged."

2. *v.* 8: "Naftali" comes from a word meaning "to twist up against something." This is descriptive of the struggle between the sisters for bearing Yakov sons, and their vying for his approval and love.

3. *v.* 11: The word *gad* in Hebrew means "luck" or "fortune"; perhaps in this context it is best understood as matching a modern day concept of "blessing."

13 So Leah said, "I'm happy because of these girls" (domestic servants), so she named him Asher.[4]

14 During the time of the wheat harvest, Reuven went and found aphrodisiac plants in a field, and he brought them to Leah, his mother. So Rachel said to Leah, "Please give your son's aphrodisiac plants to me."[5]

15 She replied to her, "It was enough that you took my husband. Do you want to take my son's aphrodisiac plants, too?" Rachel answered, "Okay, you can sleep with him tonight in exchange for your son's plants."

16 So when Yakov returned from the field in the evening, Leah met him and she said, "You will have sexual relations with *me* as a result of the deal for my son's aphrodisiac plants." And he slept with her that very night.

17 And God listened to Leah, so she got pregnant and bore a fifth son to Yakov.

18 Then Leah said, "God has rewarded me, because I gave my domestic servant to my husband." She named him Yissakar.

19 Leah conceived again and gave birth to a sixth son for Yakov.[6]

20 So Leah said, "Now God has given me a good present. My husband will be intimate with me because I bore him six sons." And so she named him Zevulun.[7]

21 Afterwards, she gave birth to a daughter and named her Dinah.[8]

---

4. *v.* 13: The name *asher* derives from the root word for happiness.

5. *v.* 14: If I am identifying this plant correctly, it is the *mandragora officinarum*, or *luffa* in Arabic. The Hebrew word used, *duda'im*, means something akin to "love-plant," and I am guessing that it was used as an aphrodisiac. Perhaps it is akin to the use of *gat*, the Yemenite aphrodisiac mix that is made up of plants. Being that Rachel, who asks for the plant, is the one who had yet to bear children, it makes contextual sense that *duda'im* were aphrodisiac plants.

6. *v.* 19: The name *Yissakar* is derived from the root "s-k-r," meaning "to reward" someone.

7. *v.* 20: Meaning "living place, abode, a place where one spends time," and referring to the fact that now Leah hoped that Yakov would spend his conjugal time with her.

8. *v.* 21: This name is the feminine equivalent of Dan, meaning "God has judged" (the given situation).

22 Then God remembered Rachel and heard her plea. God opened up her womb.

23 So she became pregnant and gave birth to a son, saying, "God has removed my shame."

24 She named him Joseph, saying: "God has added to me yet another son."[9]

25 When Rachel gave birth to Joseph, Yakov said to Lavan, "Send me off, so I can go to my permanent home and to my Land.

26 Give me my wives and my children, since I've worked for you in exchange for them. Then I'll leave, since you know how long and hard I've worked for you."

27 So Lavan said to him, "If you care for me, (stay with me); I have determined that God has blessed me because of you."

28 Then he said, "Figure out your wages, and I'll give them to you."

29 And he (Yakov) responded to him, "You know how I've worked for you, and how your animals have done under my supervision.

30 The little that you had before I came here has become much. God has blessed you because of me. So now, when will I have the chance to head my own family?"

31 He answered, "What can I give you?," to which Yakov responded, "Don't give me anything. Instead, do what I ask and I'll continue to shepherd and watch over your sheep.

32 I will inspect each of your sheep today. I'll take away every spotted and marked one, and every brown lamb, as well as the marked and spotted goats. These will be my wages.

33 Every goat that I possess that is not spotted or marked, along with every lamb that is not brown, will be considered stolen. Tomorrow you can come and inspect, and see how honest (a system) this is when you come to assess my wages."

34 Lavan responded, "Okay, let's do exactly what you say."

9. *v.* 24: That is, she now has her own son, in addition to the sons of her domestic servant, which were counted in her part of the family. Joseph's Hebrew name, "Yosef," means "added" or "additional."

35 So on that same day, he (Lavan) removed the spotted and marked male goats, as well as all the striped, marked, and brown goats that had white coloring, and put them under the care of his own sons.

36 Then he put three days' space between himself and Yakov. And Yakov shepherded Lavan's remaining flocks.

37 Yakov took for himself fresh, moist branches of the white poplar tree, and he peeled them so that the white that was on the branches could be seen.

38. Then he stuck the branches that he had peeled into the water hole where the sheep came to drink, right where they would drink. The female sheep were in heat as they came to drink.

39 The sheep mated by the branches, and they bore lambs that were spotted, striped, and marked.

40 So Yakov put these lambs aside, while he lined up Lavan's striped and brown sheep. He separated these flocks by themselves and did not mix them with (the rest of) Lavan's sheep.

41 When the mature female sheep were in heat, Yakov put the branches in the sheeps' water springs in the water pool, so they could mate by the branches.[10]

42 But he did not put the immature sheep (in the mating area). So the immature sheep were Lavan's, while the mature sheep belonged to Yakov.

43 So the man (Yakov) became very prosperous, since he had large numbers of sheep, female servants and male servants, plus camels and donkeys.

---

10. v. 41: The word *ayin*, rendered by me as "water springs," also means "eye" in Hebrew, and so could refer to a physical position ("eye to eye" or "in front of") as opposed to a water spring. Other translations prefer such a rendering (e.g., the Targum).

Chapter 31

1   (Yakov) heard that Lavan's sons were accusing him by saying, "Yakov took everything that our father owns and has gotten rich by taking advantage of our father's prosperity."

2   Yakov recognized that Lavan's demeanor toward him was not as warm as it had been in better times.

3   So God said to Yakov, "Return to the land of your fathers, to your homeland, and I will be with you."

4   Then Yakov sent for Rachel and Leah to come out to the field where his sheep (were).

5   And he said to them, "I see the look on your father's face. It isn't the same as it was before. Now, the God of my father has been with me.

6   I'm sure you know that I worked for your father with all my might.

7   But your father treated me without respect and changed my wages ten times. Yet God did not let him seriously harm me.

8   If he said, 'The spotted (sheep) will be your wages,' then all the sheep were born striped. If he said, 'The striped (sheep) will be your wages,' then all the sheep were born spotted.

9   so God marked off, then gave me your father's livestock.

10 During mating season, when the sheep were in heat, I had a dream where the male goats were mating with females that had stripes, were spotted, and were marked.

11 Then the messenger angel of God said to me in the dream, 'Yakov!' I answered, 'I'm right here!'

12 Then he said, 'Look out there! All the male goats that are mating have stripes and spots; they are marked, because I understand all that Lavan has done.

13 I am the God of Bet-El, for Whom you anointed a memorial stone when you made a vow to me there. Now, get up and leave from this land, and return to the Land of your birth.'

14 So Rachel and Leah answered and said to him, "Don't we still have some part in the inheritance of our father's estate?

15 Because he sold us, doesn't this show that he thinks of us as foreigners? And hasn't he spent *our* money?

16 All of the wealth that God has removed from our father is rightfully ours and our children's. So, all that God has told you to do, do it!"

17 Then Yakov rose up and put his sons and his wives on camels.

18 He brought all of his livestock and household goods that he had acquired or bought in Padam Aram, so that he could go to Isaac his father, in the Land of Canaan.

19 Afterwards, Lavan went to shear his sheep, and it was then that Rachel stole cultic objects that belonged to her father.[1]

20 So Yakov gave Lavan the Aramean what was due to him—he vanished without telling him!

21 He fled, taking everything that belonged to him. Then he crossed the (Jordan) River, and set out for Mount Gilad.

22 On the third day, Lavan was told that Yakov had fled.

23 So he took his brothers with him and pursued Yakov. Seven days into the pursuit, he caught up with him at Mount Gilad.

24 But God came to Lavan the Aramean in a dream in the night, and said to him, "Be careful not to speak nastily to Yakov, but nicely."

---

1. *v.*19: The word that I translated as "cultic objects" is *teraphim*. It has many possible definitions, indicating that we do not know for certain what this word meant. The objects may have been carved wooden idols or some type of occult religious object. The Targum Yerushalmi indicates that *teraphim* were made of human body parts, but this is not a commonly accepted definition. For further discussion about the definition, I refer the reader to the excellent short article on this word that is found at: http://www.jewish encyclopedia.com/view.jsp?artid=150&letter=T.

25 Then Lavan overtook Yakov, who pitched his tent at the foot of the mountain. So Lavan and his brothers also pitched their camp at Mount Gilad.

26 Finally, Lavan said to Yakov, "What did you do to me? You wronged me, and left with my daughters like they were booty from war!

27 Why did you conceal your plans to suddenly leave, and do me wrong by not telling me? I would have gladly sent you off with joyful songs, drumming and stringed music.

28 You didn't even let me kiss my grandsons and my daughters! Now, look at what you did!

29 I have it in my power to harm you, but the God of your fathers spoke to me last night and said, 'Be careful not to speak nastily to Yakov, but nicely.'

30 But why did you steal my idols?"

31 Then Yakov answered and said to Lavan, "I feared and believed that you would forcibly take your daughters away from me.

32 If by chance you find your idols, the thief should not live in the presence of our family. Look and see what I have, and take what you will." However, Yakov did not know that Rachel had stolen them.

33 So Lavan entered Yakov's tent, Leah's tent and that of the two domestic servants (Zilpah and Bilhah). Nothing was found. Then Leah left the tent and entered Rachel's tent.

34 And Rachel took the cultic objects and put them inside her camel riding pillow. She then sat on them. Lavan searched the entire tent but didn't find anything.

35 Speaking to her father, she said, "Don't become angry, sir, but I can't get up to greet you; I'm having cramps." So he looked around but didn't find any cultic objects.

36 Then he became angry at Yakov, who fought with Lavan. Yakov answered him, saying to Lavan: "What crime have I committed? What wrong did I do, that you carried out such a manhunt for me?

37 Now that you have inspected all of my goods, did you find any of your possessions? If so, put them in front of my family and yours, and they can judge between the two of us.

38 It's been twenty years that I have been with you! I have not taken your ewes or your goats, and I have not eaten the rams of your flocks!

39 Never did I bring you meat torn from wild animals. I took the loss myself for whatever was missing. It was me who was stolen from, day and night!

40 Searing heat consumed me by day, and freezing cold at night; sleep was elusive.

41 This was my life for the past twenty years in your household. I served you fourteen years for both of your daughters and six years for your flock. And you changed my wages on ten occasions!

42 If the God of my father, the God of Avraham and the Feared One of Isaac, wasn't with me, you would have sent me home empty-handed, in poverty and without anything. But God saw my plight, and so He rebuked you last night!"

43 Then Lavan answered, saying to Yakov: "The girls are my daughters, and their sons are my sons, and the flocks are my flocks. All that you see is mine! What should I do with all of them today, or with their sons to whom they gave birth?

44 So, let's go now and make a covenant between you and me. It will be a witness (of legal affairs) between you and me."[2]

45 Yakov then took a rock and set it up as a memorial marker.

46 And Yakov said to his family, "Scatter rocks on the ground," and they took rocks and made a rock pile. Then they ate at the rock pile.

47 Lavan called it "Yegar Shahaduta"; Yakov named it "Galed."[3]

---

2. *v.* 44: Dr. David Elgavish of Bar-Ilan University identifies the "witness" not as the treaty itself, but as either God Himself or the memorial marker and the pile of stones. You can find his excellent article "Jacob's Treaty with Laban" at http://www.biu.ac.il/JH/ Parasha/eng/ vayetze/elga.html.

3. *v.* 47: The names given to this site are insightful: *Yegar sahaduta* (Laban's appellation) is an Aramaic phrase meaning "testimony mound"; *Galed* (Yakov's appellation) in Hebrew means "witness pile." Both names inform us that the rock pile was a "witness"; i.e. a memorial or reminder, of the agreement made between these men.

48 So Lavan stated, "This pile is a witness between me and you today. Because of this, its name is 'Galed,'

49 as well as 'Outlook Point,' since God will see everything that is between me and you when we are hidden from each other's sight.

50 If you treat my daughters poorly, or if you marry other women besides my daughters, none of us will see it. Yet God will be Witness between me and you."

51 Lavan then said to Yakov, "Look, remember this pile and the Outlook Point that I set up between you and me!

52 This pile and the Outlook Point are witnesses that I will not cross them to come towards you, and you will not cross them to come over toward me and do evil.

53 May the God of Avraham, the God of Nachor and the God of their father judge between us!" So Yakov swore an oath through the Feared One of his father Isaac.[4]

54 So Yakov sacrificed an offering at the mountain. He summoned his family to eat a meal, and they ate, then slept the night at the mountain.

---

4. *v.* 53: The "Feared One" is a name in this verse for God.

Chapter 32

1 Lavan woke up early in the morning, kissed his grandsons and his daughters, and blessed them. Then he left to return to his home. Then Yakov went on his way, when the messenger-angels of God met him.

2 When he saw them, Yakov said, "This is the camp of God," and he named this site "Two Camps."

3 Afterward, Yakov sent out messengers into the land of Seir, in the plains of Edom, to his brother Esav.

4 He gave them orders, saying, "Say these words to my master, to Esav: 'This is what your servant Yakov has to say: I lived with Lavan, staying there until now.

5 Now I have bulls, donkeys, flocks of sheep and male and female servants. I am sending (this message) to bring news to my master, and to find your favor.'"

6 The messengers returned to Yakov, and said, "We went to your brother Esav, and he is coming to meet you along with four hundred men!"

7 So Yakov became quite afraid and was in distress. He divided the clan that was with him, along with the flocks, cattle and camels into two camps.

8 He said, "If Esav comes to the first camp and attacks it, then the remaining camp can flee."[1]

9 Then Yakov prayed, "God of my father Avraham, and God of my father Isaac, God, Who said to me, 'Return to your Land, to your motherland, and I will make it go well for you,'

---

1. v. 8: Dr. David Elgavish of Bar-Ilan University notes that "Jacob behaved with astute diplomacy in appeasing Esau, by treating Esau as a subject relates to his king. Jacob sent malakhim, meaning messengers but denoting a more elevated status than 'servants.' . .Jacob prostrated himself before Esau seven times (33.3). Seven-fold prostration from afar expresses submission to a king. . . . Why did Jacob behave in this subservient manner to Esau? His objective was to appear before Esau as one for whom no blessings had been fulfilled." In this way, Yakov's subservient status to Esav would have been obvious to all and would result in the mitigating of any revenge.

10 I am humbled by all of the kindnesses and the truth that You have carried out for Your servant. I have crossed the Jordan River on foot and now I am divided into two groups.

11 Please save me from my brother Esav's hand, because I fear him, as he can come and strike both mother and child.

12 It is You Who said that 'I will work things for your favor,' and 'I will make your descendants as the sand of the sea that due to its great number can't be counted.'"

13 So he slept there that night, and took from the goods that he had brought to prepare a gift for Esav his brother:

14 two hundred female goats and twenty male goats, along with two hundred ewes and twenty rams;

15 thirty female camels that were suckling their young, forty cows, ten bulls, twenty female donkeys, and then young donkeys.

16 Then he gave his servants each herd, one by one, and said to his servants: "Go forward, in front of me, and make sure there is some distance between each herd."

17 And he commanded the lead (servant), saying, "When Esav my brother meets up with you, and asks, 'who do you belong to?', 'where are you going?', and 'whose (herd) is this moving forward?'

18 tell him, 'it belongs to your servant Yakov, and it's a gift that is being sent to my master Esav. And look, he is in back of us!'"

19 He also commanded the same to the second and third servants, as well as all those who followed the herds, saying, "Say exactly the same thing to Esav when you find him.

20 You must also say, 'Look, your servant Yakov is behind us,'" because he thought, "I will calm him down with the gift that is being brought in front of me; afterwards, he will act kindly."

21 And the gift went on before him. He slept that night in the camp.

22 He got up that very night and took both of his wives along with his two domestic servants and his eleven children. Then he crossed over the Yabbok ford.

23 So he took them and crossed over the river, bringing his possessions.[2]

24 Yakov left off from everyone, and then a man grappled with him till the first light of dawn.

25 Since he (the man) saw that he could not overpower him (Yakov), he hit him (Yakov) in his hip socket. Yakov's hip was dislocated in this struggle with him.

26 Then the (man) said, "Let me go! It's already dawn." He (Yakov) replied, "I won't let you go unless you bless me!"

27 So he (the man) replied to him, "What's your name?" And he said, "Yakov."

28 Then he stated, "You won't be named Yakov any longer, but Israel, because you struggled with God and with men and you won!"

29 And Yakov asked a question, saying, "Please tell me your name." So he (the man) said, "Why are you asking for my name?", but he did bless him there.[3]

30 So Yakov called the name of the place "The face of God," because "I saw God face-to-face and my life was spared."

31 The sun rose as he went on from Penuel, and he limped because of his hip.[4]

---

2. v. 23–25: The name Yakov, the Yabbok River, and the verb "to struggle" (with the unidentified man) all form a word play in Hebrew. Yakov, Yabbok, and ye'avek are the three words used in these verses, and they sound alike, giving a playful emphasis (and a pneumonic memorization device) to this story. Literally, Yakov crosses the Yabbok, and his name (Yakov) gets scrambled to form the verb that describes what happened . . . that is, the word "to fight" is ye'avek which scrambles a few of the letters of the name Yakov. Physically, Yakov's body, like his name, was scrambled up a bit in the fight against the man (i.e., the dislocated hip).

3. v. 29: There may be a double pun here, in that Yakov's new name is related to struggling with God and men, yet also to reigning with God and men. Sar, the root of the name Israel, is also a "prince" or "ruler" in ancient Hebrew. Thus, Yakov's name change does denote his struggles, and also reflects on the fact that he won his struggles of both a human and heavenly nature. Thus, he has a princely position with God (sar-el, equaling a "prince with God.")

4. v. 31: The name "Peni'el," is translated as "Face of God" and is the name given to this place.

32 Because of this incident, till today the people of Israel do not eat the sciatic nerve that is embedded in the thigh, since Yakov's thigh was hit right on his sciatic nerve.[5]

5. v. 32 "Penu'el" is nearly the same word in Hebrew as the aforementioned "Peniel." Commentators state that it is the same place, with possibly a later Hebrew name (Penu'el) being used instead of the older name (Peni'el) of v. 31. Perhaps the difference in spelling and pronunciation between these two names reflects a difference in tribal accents, with Penu'el becoming the standard pronunciation at a later time. At any rate, Peni'el and Penu'el are variant spellings of the same place, and both are used in our text here in Bereshit. Renowned Rabbi Shlomo Breuer (d. 1926) explained the difference in a midrashic, homiletic manner: "When Yaakov meets Esav at night, and succeeds, he calls it Pen-i-el. This is the face of God. But when the dawn arrives and we get the 'brotherly love' of Esav, then it is Pen-u-el, meaning 'penu-el'—God clears away, He leaves. When one is fighting and must struggle with Esav, one can be assured of Peniel—the Face of God is present" (http://www.torah.org/learning/ravfrand/ 5757/vayishlach.html). Rabbi Breuer (1850–1926), was one of the founders of the Agudat Yisrael movement in Germany. His son was Rabbi Joseph, who courageously fled Nazi Germany with his synagogue members after Reichskristallnacht ("Crystal Night") in 1938, and resettled in New York City. As background for understanding Rabbi Breuer's comment, the rabbis write that Yakov fought with Esav or with Esav's angel in chapter 32's wrestling match. Thus, Yakov was struggling against his brother, in one manner or another. "Peni-el" means "face of God," while as Rabbi Breuer writes, "Penu-el" can mean "God vacated (a place)," from the Hebrew verb lefanot (to vacate, to leave).

Chapter 33

1   Then Yakov looked out in the distance and saw that Esav was coming, and four hundred men were with him. So he divided up the children of Leah, Rachel and the two domestic servants.

2   He put the domestic servants and their children first (in formation), then Leah and her children after them, and finally Rachel with Joseph in the rear.

3   After this, he went before them, prostrating himself on the ground seven times until he came to his brother.

4   Then Esav ran toward him to meet him, embraced him with heartfelt passion, and kissed him, crying.[1]

5   He (Esav) looked into the distance and saw the wives and children, then said: "How are these people related to you?" So he responded, "These are the children whom God has graciously given to your servant."

6   Afterward, the domestic servants came to him (Esav) along with their children, and prostrated themselves on the ground.

7   Leah also came, accompanied by her children, and they prostrated themselves, after which Joseph and Rachel came, also prostrating themselves.

8   So he (Esav) said: "What is the purpose of me meeting this entire camp?" He (Yakov) answered, "To gain your favor."

9   And Esav said, "I have plenty, my brother. What you have remains yours."

10 Yakov replied, "No, please, I ask you to receive my gift, if I have found favor with you. Meeting you is like being in God's presence, and this will show that you are satisfied with me.

---

1. *v.* 4: The Hebrew phrase *vayipol 'al tsavaro* is difficult to translate (lit. "to fall on his neck"). However, it relays emotion that is between these twin brothers as they have an intimate moment. This does not, however, change the status of Esav (cf. Malachi 1.3 ". . . and Esav I have hated"). Jewish thought historically assesses Esav's character to have been evil, and his Edomite descendants as enemies of Israel (cf. the book of Obadiah and the figure of Haman in Esther 3.1).

11 So please take the blessing that I have brought for you, because God has been good to me, and I have everything. Because he (Yakov) pressed him, he (Esav) took it."

12 Then he (Esav) said, "Let's leave here and be on our way. I'll travel along with you."

13 He (Yakov) replied to him, "Sir, you know that the children are immature and weak, and the sheep and cattle need my attention. All the sheep will die if they are pushed hard another day.

14 Please, let my master go on ahead of his servant, while I proceed ahead slowly, alongside both the herds and the children until I catch up with my master by Seir."

15 Then Esav said, "Allow me to leave you with some of my clan that are with me." But he (Yakov) responded, "But why? I only want to find favor with you."

16 On that very day, Esav went on his way toward Seir.

17 So Yakov traveled toward Sukkot, and built a shelter for himself and pens for his cattle. He named the place "Sukkot."[2]

18 Later, Yakov arrived in peace to the city of Shechem that is in the land of Canaan, on his journey from Padan-Aram. He camped facing the city.

19 He bought a parcel of land where he had pitched his tent from the sons of Hamor, the father of Shechem, for 100 *kasitas*.[3]

2. *v. 17*: The word *sukkot* in Hebrew, while being a geographic place name, also refers to a hut, temporary shelter, or a structure built for celebration of the holiday of Sukkot. In this verse, since it is being used for structures that are in reference to sheep and cattle, I imagine that pens and sheepfolds are being described.

3. *v. 19*: "Hamor," though here a proper name, means "ass" or "donkey" in Hebrew, perhaps a humorous assessment of the given man's character. A *kasita* is either a type of currency or a means of payment. The Targum believed it to be payment via lambs (live animals). I refer the reader to an informative short article on the kasita by Dr. Zohar Amar of Bar-Ilan University, which is found at http://www.biu.ac.il/JH/Parasha/eng/vay-ishlach/vayish1.html. *v. 20*: Most translations have Yakov giving a name to the altar that he erected (". . . he called it God, the God of Israel" CJB). However, I prefer to translate the word *lo* not as "it" but as "to Him"; that is, to God, the God of Israel. In other words, it is clear that Yakov would have worshipped God at the altar (as reads the translation of the Targum). It is true that there are other ways to state the same, and my rendition reads a bit bluntly, yet I favor it because of the verse's intent and context.

20 Then he erected an altar there and he called upon God, the God of Israel.

Chapter 34

1   Leah's daughter Dinah, who was born to Yakov, went to visit the young women of the area.

2   Shechem the son of Hamor, the Hivite ruler of the area, saw her, and he laid with her and raped her.

3   He fell for Dinah, Yakov's daughter, loved the young woman, and spoke with tenderness to her.

4   So Shechem talked with Hamor, his father, saying, "Get this girl for me as my wife."

5   Then Yakov heard that Dinah his daughter had been defiled. His sons were tending the cattle in the field, and Yakov kept silent until they came home.

6   Shechem's father Hamor went to Yakov in order to talk to him.

7   When Yakov's sons returned from the field, they heard them (Yakov and Hamor) talking. They were saddened and very angry that such an evil deed had been perpetrated against Israel: Yakov's daughter had been raped, and he hadn't done anything about it!

8   So Hamor spoke with them, saying, "Shechem my son has fallen madly in love with the young lady. Please give her to him as his wife.[1]

9   And then you can intermarry with us; you can give us your young ladies to marry, and we'll give you ours.

10   You'll live with us, and the whole land can be for your use. Settle where you want, conduct your business, and go ahead and take whatever land you need."

11   Then Shechem said to her father and brothers, "You will like me, and whatever you say to me, you will have.

---

1. *v.* 1: The Hivites were a Canaanite nation whose territory was in the north central part of Israel. In a later time period, when Yehoshua (Joshua) entered the Land with the tribes of Israel, the Hivites occupied four cities: Giv'on, Chapirah, Be'erot and Kiryat-Ye'arim.

12 Go ahead and set a high bride price and dowry, and I'll give what you ask of me. Then, you'll give me the young woman for my wife."

13 Jacob's sons answered Shechem and his father Hamor dishonestly when they spoke, because he had violated their sister Dinah.

14 They said to them, "We can't do this; we can't give our sister in marriage to anyone who is not circumcised, because that is disgraceful to us.

15 However, we can agree under one condition; if every male among you becomes like us by getting circumcised.

16 Then we'll give our young women to you, and we'll take your young women for us. We'll live with you, and we'll all be one nation.

17 But if you won't cooperate with us and get circumcised, we'll take our young lady and leave."

18 But Hamor and his son Shechem were pleased with their offer.

19 The young man (Shechem) did not hesitate to go through with this, because he greatly desired the daughter of Yakov. He was the most honored person in all of his family.

20 So Hamor and his son Shechem went to the city gate, and spoke with the men of the city, saying:

21 "These people are perfectly suited for us, and will settle in the land; they'll do their business here, since the land has enough room for them. We'll take their young women for wives, and we'll give them our young women.

22 But there is one condition to be met before these people will settle with us in order to make one nation--every male of ours needs to be circumcised like they are circumcised.

23 Won't all their cattle, possessions and animals become ours? So, let's cooperate with them, and they'll live among us."

24 And all these men left the city gate, accepting what Hamor and his son Shechem said. So every male of his city was circumcised.

25 On the third day afterwards, they (the men of Shechem) were in pain. Shimon and Levi, the two sons of Yakov and brothers of Dinah, came with their swords to the off-guard city, and killed every male.

26 They killed Hamor and his son Shechem with their swords, and took Dinah away from Shechem's house. Then they left.

27 Yakov's sons took the possessions of the dead men of this city that had violated their sister.

28 They took their sheep, their cattle and their donkeys as well as goods from the city itself, and items from the surrounding fields;

29 this included all their weapons; as well, their children and their wives were also taken captive. They plundered household items from the houses, too.[2]

30 Then Yakov said to Shimon and Levi, "You've brought great shame upon me in the eyes of this land's inhabitants--the Canaanites and the Perizzites. I am a few in number, so that if they join forces against me and fight me, I will be destroyed, both me and my family!"

31 And they responded, "Should our sister be treated like a whore?"[3]

2. *v.* 8: The phrase "your daughter" is referred to in the plural possessive in the text. Thus, this word could be rendered "your young lady," and be in reference to Dinah, the "young lady" of the family. This would make sense with the usage of "you" in the plural (as if Hamor was speaking to Yakov *and* his sons, since Hamor "spoke with *them*" in v. 8a).

3. *v.* 29: I translated the Hebrew word '*chayl*' here as "weapons." A typical understanding of '*chayl*' is connected to military life, and I favor this interpretation from the context of the text. Other translations view the word as referring to "treasures," "wealth" (JPS), "everything they owned" (CJB), "plunder" (NET), and "personal possessions" (Targum).

Chapter 35

1 So God said to Yakov, "Get up, go to Bet-El, and live there. Make an altar to God there, the One Who appeared to you when you fled from your brother Esav."

2 Yakov then told his family and all those who were with him, "Throw away the foreign idols that are in your possession and purify yourselves. Change your garments.

3 Then we'll get up and go up to Bet-El. I'll make an altar there to God, the One Who answers me on the day of my distress, since He is with me on the road that I travel."

4 So they gave Yakov all of their foreign idols that they had with them and all their earrings, and Yakov buried them under the terebinth tree that was at nearby Shechem.

5 Then as they traveled, the fear of God fell on the cities that were around them. So no one pursued Jacob's clan.

6 Yakov came toward Luz (also called. Bet-El), in the land of Canaan, with his entire clan.

7 And he built an altar there, calling the place 'God, the God of Bet-El,' because God was revealed to him there, when he fled from his brother.

8 Rivkah's wetnurse, Devorah, died and was buried at Bet-El under the oak tree. The site was named "the tree of weeping."

9 Then God appeared to Yakov once again, on his return from Paddan-Aram, and He blessed him.

10 God said to him, "Although your name is Yakov, you will no longer be called by your name 'Yakov,' because Israel is your name." And He called his name Israel.

11 So God said to him, "I am Almighty God. Reproduce and be numerous; a people consisting of a community of tribes, as well as kings, will descend from you."

12 I give to you and to your descendants the land that I gave to Avraham and Isaac; I will give the land (to you).

13 At the very place where He spoke to him, God then left him.

14 Yakov set up a memorial in the place where (God) spoke with Him. It was a memorial marker made of stone, over which he poured a water libation, after which he poured oil on it.

15 So Yakov named the place where God spoke with him, "Bet-El."[1]

16 Then the clan traveled from Bet-El, and while they were some distance from arriving at Efrata, Rachel entered into hard labor and gave birth.

17 While she was having difficulty in giving birth, her midwife said to her, "Don't fear, because now you have another son!"

18 She named him "Ben-oni," and then she died. But his father called him "Binyamin."[2]

19 So Rachel (of blessed memory) died and was buried on the road to Efrata, at Bethlehem.[3]

20 Yakov set up a memorial stone at her tomb, which is the stone at Rachel's tomb till today.

21 So Israel traveled on, and pitched his tent just beyond the guard tower for the animals.[4]

---

1. *v.* 15: "Bet El" in Hebrew means "house of God," and is a town in modern-day Israel, as well.

2. *v.* 18: "Ben-oni" means 'son of my pain," while "Binyamin" means "beloved son" or "favored son.." Literally, Binyamin means "son of my right hand." This idiom "the right hand" was the ancient term for the place where one's favorite guest would be seated, as well as one's favorite son (perhaps at meals or meetings). For example, Psalm 110 reads, "sit at my right hand until I make your enemies your footstool." If this verse is interpreted messianically, then the "right hand" is the place of greatest favor and honor, reserved for the Messiah.

3. *v.* 19: The town of Efrat is the same as Efrata. Both names are used in referring to the same place.

4. *v.* 21: The site is called "Migdal Eder" ("Herd Tower") in Hebrew, and was a place where animal pens and a tower must have existed for use by shepherds. Sometimes a small stone tower was erected at the corner of animal pens to watch over them from their enemies and from thieves.

22 During Israel's stay in this Land, Reuven had sexual relations with Bilha, his father's concubine, and Israel found out about it. All told, Jacob had twelve sons.[5]

23 The sons of Leah were Yakov's firstborn son, Reuven, and Shimon, Levi, Yehudah, Yissachar, and Zevulun.

24 Rachel's sons were Joseph and Binyamin.

25 The sons of Bilha, Rachel's domestic servant, were Dan and Naftali.

26 The sons of Zilpa, Leah's domestic servant, were Gad and Asher. These were Yakov's sons who were born to him in Paddan-Aram.

27 Yakov arrived to see his father Isaac at Mamre (Kiryat Arba), which is Hevron, where Avraham and Isaac had both lived.

28 Isaac lived to be 180 years old.

29 Then Isaac died and passed away. He was an elderly and aged man when his family buried him. It was Esav, along with Yakov and his sons, who buried him.

---

5. *v.* 22: In the ancient world, a "concubine" (Hebrew *pilagesh*) was a woman who had conjugal relations with a man but was not legally married to him. Yet she could be a member of his family. Sanhedrin 21a defines this category for us in stating: "Rav Yehudah taught (that) Rav taught: 'wives were women with a *ketubah* (marriage certificate), and with a marriage ceremony; '*pilgeshim*' were without a ketubah and marriage ceremony." In this Talmudic verse, "Rav" refers to Abba Arika, the Babylonian Jewish sage who founded the famous Sura yeshiva (d. 247 a.d.). My book *Who Knows Abba Arika* deals in small part with his life and influence in Jewish history (Shoreshim Publications). *Pilgeshim* is the plural form of *pilagesh*. Rav Yehudah is correctly identified as Yehudah ben Yehezkel (d. 299 a.d.), one of the leading students of Abba Arika. In this verse, Yehudah quotes the teaching of his rabbi, Abba Arika.

Chapter 36

1 This is the family history of Esav, the father of the Edomites.

2 Esav took his wives from the Canaanite women: Adah the daughter of Elon the Hittite, and Ohalivama the daughter of Anah, and grand-daughter of Sevon the Hivite;

3 Basmat the daughter of Ishmael, the sister of Neviyot.

4 Adah gave birth to Elifaz, which added to Esav's clan; Basmat gave birth to Reu'el.

5 Then Ohalivama gave birth to Ye'ish, Ya'lam, and Korach. These were the sons of Esav that were born to him in the land of Canaan.

6 So Esav took his wives and his sons and daughters, and all of his clan, as well as his cattle and his beasts of burden, and his personal property that he had acquired in the land of Canaan. Then he went to an area that was further away from his brother Yakov.

7 This was because their possessions were too great for them to live to-gether. The place where they lived was not able to support (both of) them because of the number of their cattle.

8 So Esav lived near Mt. Seir. Esav was the father of the Edomites.

9 This is the family history of Esav, progenitor of the Edomites, from Mt. Seir.

10 These are the names of Esav's sons: Elifaz, son of Adah, Esav's wife; Reu'el, son of Basmat, Esav's wife.

11 Elifaz's sons were Teman, Omer, Safo, Ga'tem, and Kenaz.

12 Timna was the concubine of Esav's son Elifaz. She gave birth to Amalek, for the clan of Elifaz.

13 These are the sons of Reu'el: Nachat, Zerach, Shammah, and Mizah. They were the descendants of Basmat, Esav's wife.

14 These were the sons of Ohalivama, wife of Esav and daughter of Anah and granddaughter of Sivon. She gave birth to Ye'ish, Ya'lam, and Korach.

15 The following men were the warriors among Esav's descendants. From Elifaz, the firstborn son of Esav: Teman was a warrior, Omer was a warrior, Sefo was a warrior, and Kenaz was a warrior.

16 Korach was a warrior, Ga'tem was a warrior, and Amalek was a warrior. These were the warriors among Elifaz's clan in the land of Edom; these were all Adah's sons.

17 Among the sons of Esav's son Reu'el: Nachat was a warrior, Zerach was a warrior, Shamma was a warrior, and Mizah was a warrior. These were the warriors among the clan of Reu'el in the land of Edom. They were descendants of Esav's wife, Basmat.

18 Among the sons of Esav's wife Ohalivama, Ye'ush was a warrior.

19 These were the descendants of Esav along with their warriors. They made up the Edomites.

20 The following were the descendants of Seir the Horite, living in the land: Lotan, Shoval, Sivon, and Anah;

21 Dishon, Etzer, and Dishan. They were the warriors of the Horites, descendants of Seir, in the land of Edom.

22 The sons of Lotan were Hori, Hemam, Achot, Lotan, and Timna.

23 The descendants of Shoval were Alvan, Manachat, Eyval, Shafo, and Onam.[1]

24 The descendants of Sivon were Ayyah, and Anah, who found hot springs in the desert as he was looking after his father Sivon's donkeys.[2]

---

1. *v.* 23: Interestingly enough, "Manachat" is the name of a current Jerusalem neighborhood, with the same spelling in modern Hebrew.

2. *v.* 24: The Hebrew word here for "hot springs" (*hayemim*) is a bit obscure. However, as both the JPS and Targum render the word to be hot springs, I am thus following suit. The Syriac translation renders this as "water was discovered" in lieu of hot springs. Given the geography and water tables of the Middle East, this is certainly noteworthy on its own, whether the water was thermal, from an artesian well, or not. Two prominent rabbinic commentators identify *hayemim* as "giants" (Ramban, Ibn Ezra), akin to the later *anakim* that Yehoshua and Calev encountered in Israel, or that David defeated in the battle against the Philistines (cf. Numbers 13.28,33,1 Samuel 17.4). Another translation

25 Anah had a son, Dishon, and a daughter, Ohalivama.

26 Hemdan, Eshban, Yitran, and Karan were Dishon's sons.

27 Bilhan, Za'avan, and Akan were Etzer's sons.

28 Utz and Aran were the sons of Dishan.

29 The Horite warriors were Lotan, Shoval, Sivon, Anah,

30 Dishon, Etzer, and Dishan. They were the Horite warriors, heads of their fighting men in the land of Seir.

31 There were kings who ruled in the land of Edom, before the days of a king in Israel.

32 Bela the son of Be'or from the city of Dinhava ruled as king.

33 When Bela died, Yovav son of Zerach from Botzrah, reigned in his stead.

34 When Yovav died, Husham from the land of Yemen reigned in his stead.

35 When Husham died, Hadad son of Bedad from Avit reigned in his stead. He defeated the Midianites in the fields of Moab.

36 When Hadad died, Samlah from Masrekah ruled in his stead.

37 When Samlah died, then Shaul from the town of Rehovot, next to the river, ruled.

38 When Shaul died, the tribal chief Hanan son of Akbor ruled as king.

39 When the chieftain Hanan son of Akbor died, Hadar from Pa'u, whose wife was Mehitavel daughter of Matrer and granddaughter of Mey-Zahav, ruled as king.

---

is worded as follows: "[Anah] discovered [how to breed] mules in the desert when he was tending the donkeys for his father Tziv'on" (taken from http://bible.ort.org/books/Torahd5.asp?action=displayid&id=1065, "VaYishlach.") Rashi argues for this understanding. Thus the discovery that Anah makes is understood to be one in the realm of animal husbandry: by breeding donkeys and horses, he produced mules, as opposed to discovering a water source, or confronting giants like the previously mentioned offspring of the 'fallen beings'.

40 These were the warriors from the clans that descended from Esav, listed by their locale and names: Timna was a warrior, Alvah was a warrior, Yetet was a warrior;

41 Ohalivama was a warrior, Elah was a warrior, Pinon was a warrior.

42 Kenaz was a warrior, Teman was a warrior, Mivsar was a warrior.[3]

43 Magdiel was a warrior and Iram was a warrior. These were the Edomite warriors, listed by their region and by the land of their settlements. Esav the father of Edom was their progenitor.

---

3. v. 42: The word *mivsar* in Hebrew means "a military fortress."

Chapter 37

1   Yakov lived in the Land where his father had lived, in the land of Canaan.

2   This is the family history of Yakov: Joseph was seventeen years old and a shepherd of flocks, along with his brothers. He worked alongside the sons of Bilha and Zilpa, his father's concubines. And Joseph spoke very negatively about them to his father.[1]

3   But Israel loved Joseph over and above all of his sons, because he was born to him at an elderly age. So he made a striped coat for him.[2]

4   His brothers saw that of all the siblings, their father loved him the most. So they hated him so much that they were not willing to speak peacefully to him.

5   Then Joseph dreamed a dream, and he told his brothers about it. This only added to their hatred of him.

---

1. 1*v.* 2: The Torah text here gives us a strong hint that to understand the life of Yakov, we must understand his connection to his son Joseph. He loved Joseph more than life itself. The verse itself reads quite strangely; we are introduced to the *family history* of Yakov by an immediate mention *of Joseph*—"This is the family history of Yakov; *Joseph* was seventeen years old . . ." (v. 2). We may have expected something more fitting for a biography of Yakov here. However, being that Yakov possessed a passionate love for his wife Rachel, and favored her two sons, v. 2 is not a shock. Some rabbis comment that the text literally reads, ". . . and (Joseph) shepherded his brothers . . . ," which indeed is true, grammatically speaking. Much *midrash* (see glossary) can be deduced from the grammar and literal rendition of the verse. As this so touching and yet troubling narrative unfolds, indeed Joseph ends up being the "shepherd" of his entire family of origin, leading them to the only source of food that existed. In another vein, Robert Sacks wrote: "Joseph, being seventeen years old, shepherded *his* brothers among the sheep though he was a. . .(boy), that is, (among) the sons of Bilhah and the sons of Zilpah, his father's wives" (Kass, *The Beginning of Wisdom*, p. 513)). Though Rabbi Riskin also interprets this verse in this way, he sees Joseph as an arrogant youth who tries to dominate his brothers, encouraged in this by his father's favoritism (see his article "The Leaders and the Led," Parashat Vayeshev, found at http://www.jpost.com/servlet/Satellite?pagename =Jpost%2FJPArticle%2 FShowFull&cid=122 8728247474).

2. 2*v.* 3: The text infers that this striped coat was a sign of Yakov's overwhelming love and favoritism. Along with v. 2, the reader should definitely get the sense of Yakov's feelings for this particular son.

6   He had said to them, "Please, listen to the dream that I dreamed!

7   Look, we were binding sheaves in the field, and suddenly my sheave rose up and stood, and then your sheaves circled around and bowed low to my sheave!"

8   Then his brothers said to him, "So, are you going to be ruler over us? Are you going to really govern us?" As a result of his dreams and their meanings, they hated him all the more.

9   Afterward, he dreamed yet another dream, and he explained it to his brothers. He told them, "Look, I dreamed another dream, and the sun, the moon, and eleven stars were bowing down to me!"

10 He then explained it to his father and (again) to his brothers. His father rebuked him, and said to him, "What kind of dream is this that you dreamed? Am I, your mother and your brothers going to come to you, then bow down to the earth before you?"

11 So his brothers became jealous of him, but his father paid attention to the incident.

12 His brothers went to pasture the flock of their father in Shechem.

13 And Israel said to Joseph, "Since your brothers are shepherding in Shechem, I'll send you to them. Go." He (Joseph) responded to him, "I'm ready to go."

14 He instructed him, "Go now, check how your brothers are doing, and how the flocks are. Then come back to me and let me know." So he sent him (Joseph) from the Hevron Valley, and he approached Shechem.

15 A man found him there, lost in a field; so the man asked him, "What are you looking for?"

16 He responded, "I'm looking for my brothers. Can you tell me where they are shepherding?"

17 So the man told him, "Go this way, because I heard them saying, 'Let's go toward Dotan.'" And Joseph went to look for his brothers, then found them at Dotan.

18 They saw him from far off, and before he got to them, they conspired to kill him.

19 The brothers said to one another, "Look, that dreamer is coming here!

20 Now, let's go and kill him, and throw his body into one of the pits. We can say that an evil beast ate him. Then we'll see what becomes of that dreamer!"

21 Then Reuven heard about it, and saved him from the rest of them. He said, "We can't kill him!"

22 So he said to them, "Let's not shed any blood. We can throw him into this pit that's in the wilderness without harming him." He planned on saving him from them in order to return him to his father.

23 When Joseph arrived and was with his brothers, they stripped him of his striped coat that he was wearing.

24 They took him and threw him into a pit that was empty. It had no water in it.

25 Then they sat down to eat when they saw a caravan of Ishmaelites coming from Gilad, on their way down to Egypt with their camels carrying spices, balsam, and resin.

26 And Yehudah said to his brothers, "What good will it do if we kill our brother and cover up his death?

27 Let's go and sell him to these Ishmaelites, and we won't hurt him since he is our flesh and blood, our brother." So his brothers listened to him.

28 Meanwhile, Midianite merchants passed by. They (the brothers) pulled Joseph up out of the pit, and sold him to the Ishmaelites for twenty pieces of silver, and they brought Joseph into Egypt.

29 Reuven returned to the pit and since Joseph was not in it, he tore his clothes.[3]

---

3. *v.* 29: This is an ancient Middle Eastern mourning custom. It is still practiced in Jewish communities today. When a close relative dies, the family mourners must tear their garment at the funeral as a sign of grief. See also v. 34, where Yakov rends his garment after hearing about Joseph. Reuven was away when his brothers, following Yehudah's advice, sold Joseph. Thus, his reaction is as recorded. He had hoped to save Joseph from such a fate.

30 So he returned to his brothers and exclaimed "The boy is not here anymore! What am I supposed to do now?"[4]

31 They then took Joseph's coat and slaughtered a young goat, and dipped his coat in the blood.

32 They took the coat and brought it to their father, saying, "We found this. You'll have to identify whether its your son's coat or not."

33 He recognized it and said, "This is my son's coat. An evil beast has eaten him, and torn Joseph apart!"

34 So Yakov tore his garments, put sackcloth around his hips, and mourned for his son for a long time.[5]

35 All of his sons and daughters came to comfort him, but he refused to be comforted. He said, "I will die in mourning for my son," and his (Joseph's) father wailed because of him.

36 Midianites sold him to Egyptians: to Potifar, the official who was the chief of Pharaoh's chefs and his kitchen.[6]

APPENDIX TO CHAPTER 37:
THE COMPELLING LIFE OF JOSEPH

Though this work is a translation and simple commentary, I am constrained to offer some further remarks on the sheer magnanimity of this story. It is here that I always stop to admire the content of Bereshit, and

---

4. *v.* 30: As the eldest brother, Reuven has the responsibility for the well being of everyone who was present. Accordingly, he is very upset and doesn't know what to do after Joseph is sold. His hopes to return Joseph to Yakov, thereby ensuring Yakov's happiness were suddenly dashed

5. *v.* 34: It is worthwhile to mention that "Yakov" is used as his name here, when he is in a period of suffering. Earlier, he had been called "Israel" in this text (v.13). I will later comment on how the use of his names paralleled his emotional states, and his situations in life.

6. *v.* 36: I have translated the Hebrew word *tabachim* as "chefs," and by inference and logic, include "kitchen." The Targum identifies the *tabachim* as "executioners": which is a philological possibility. The root *t-b-ch* in Hebrew refers to either food preparation, or to slaughtering (usually other humans in warfare).

as so many before me have done, to marvel at the outcomes, plots, and subplots that were the crux of Joseph's life.

This is one of ancient history's most emotionally charged, humanly touching dramas. The events of Joseph's life occurred some 3,800 years ago, clearly putting it into the period of ancient Semitic literature. It is studied on a yearly basis by the Jewish world, and its myriad of lessons and wisdom, along with its depth in portraying the basic questions of life, never ceases to amaze every generation of its students. The student of Joseph's life is often in tears; some are from grief, and some are caused by sheer joy.

In some ways, Joseph's life is similar to that of his kinsmen, the Jewish people. In many periods of Jewish history, events have seemingly spun out of control, and Joseph's people found ourselves cast out of our homeland, unjustly forced into servitude, and in dire need of liberation. And then, the supernatural flow of events changed our status from victimhood to freedom, replete with independence and some political power. The events of Joseph's life, like a fixed pattern, repeat themselves throughout Jewish history time and time again. It is as if his life was meant to encapsulate all that is vital in his people's more than four thousand year history.

Simply, in Joseph, we see a mirror of Jewish history. And in Jewish history, we see a mirror of Joseph's life story. In spite of his sufferings, maltreatment, deprivations, and his sibling's abuses, he emerges as the one person whom the Almighty uses to save his own family from certain death. Additionally, Joseph is promoted into high government office, where he is honored and is second only to the Egyptian potentate. Then, he is miraculously re-united with, and restored to, his father. To complete the picture, after his death, Joseph's remains are buried in his beloved homeland, the land of Israel, according to his own instructions. His life's journey becomes one of honorable restoration through much pain.

In this biblical figure, the Jewish and Christian worlds meet in kinship. For the Christian world, as well, can sense the power of Joseph's life in a two-pronged manner. Many Christians whom I have met see in him the history of Israel and the Jewish people, as well. Further, Christian sentiments can parallel the patterns of Joseph's life to that of the Jewish rabbi, prophet and Messiah, Yeshua (Jesus). According to the gospel narratives, like the historic Jewish people, he suffered, was mistreated, misunderstood, and then severely abused at the hands of the 1st century Roman government. In Joseph's life, too, we see the pattern of redemptive trauma.

Unhappily, this same pattern is repeated too often in the history of his people, who have suffered more injustice than any other people/group in human history. And again, Israel's rabbi par excellence, Yeshua, perhaps the most influential son of Israel in all of history, also repeats this same pattern of traumatic redemption.

In Joseph's life, these themes unite, and offer Jewish and Christian communities a chance to experience a sympathetic brotherhood. This ancient story unites the Jewish and Christian worlds in hope and faith. It gives us an expectation that Israel will be restored to a place of honored service on the stage of world affairs, one in which Jewish and Christian people can share our belief in Israel's One God and express our common Judeo-Christian values. Many Christians also wait for the day in which the Church will experience a similar restoration. Joseph's story infuses me with this hope, and thus becomes a powerful purveyor of Jewish-Christian unity. Although the story's central figures disappeared eons ago from history, the hope given by this narrative remains strong.

I will conclude by saying that my perspective on the implications of Joseph's life is by no means a complete one. I welcome more insight into the meanings inherent in this text from both Jewish and Christian colleagues and students.

Chapter 38

1   In this time period, Yehudah left the family and stayed with an Adulamite man whose name was Hirah.[1]

2   While there, Yehudah saw a Canaanite woman, the daughter of Shua, and he had sexual relations with her.[2]

3   She became pregnant and bore a son, and his name was called Er.

4   Again she became pregnant and gave birth to a son and his name was called Oni.

5   Once more she was pregnant, bearing a son whom she named Shelah. She gave birth to him at Keziv.[3]

6   Yehudah then arranged for Er, his firstborn, to marry a woman whose name was Tamar.[4]

---

1. *v. 1*: Adullam was a village located southeast of Soco and northeast of Achzib, close to the Elah Valley, where King David later killed the Philistine Goliath.

2. *v. 2*: Jewish commentators do accept the literal rendering here, that the woman was a Canaanite, and alternately suggest that she was from a "merchant family" (instead of a Canaanite family). Pinner noted that: ". . . *Pesachim* 50b, *Targum Onkelos, Targum Yonatan*, Rashi, Ramban, Rashbam, Radak, the *Ohr HaChayyim*, and *Metzudat Zion* [on *Proverbs* 31.24] all render *c'na'ani* (Canaanite) in this verse as 'merchant' rather than 'Canaanite.'" I refer the reader to his commentary, "Vayeshev: In exile, redemption" found at: http://www.israelnationalnews.com/Articles/Article.aspx/8448.

3. *v. 5*: Most identify this site as Achziv, a prominent village south of Soco, in the Elah Valley.

4. *v. 6*: Logically, Yehudah would have bought Tamar from her family, according to the prescribed rites listed in Tractate Kedushin, Mishnah 1: "A woman is acquired (for marriage) by three methods, and frees herself (obtains a marriageless state) by two methods. She is acquired through money, by a legal note of obligation, and through sexual relations. . .(Kiddushin 1:1, author's translation). This is recorded as Jewish law close to 1,900 years after Yehudah's lifetime, so it is uncertain as to how much of what is in Tractate Kiddushin was practiced by Yakov and his sons. I do not know whether these marriage practices from Kiddushin 1:1 closely paralleled the accepted Canaanite rites of marriage. As well, it is unknown if Tamar's family of origin accepted the extant Jewish rites of marriage acquisition as practiced by Yakov and his sons. But here it appears that Yehudah's marriage customs are accepted by Tamar's family. Given that Yehudah had left his family and was marrying a Canaanite woman, at this point in his life, he may not have been overly concerned with his halakhic practice.

7   But Er, firstborn son of Yehudah, was judged by God to be evil. So God caused him to die.

8   Then Yehudah said to Onan, "Have sexual relations with your brother's wife, and marry her, so that your brother will have descendants."[5]

9   Onan understood that he would not be the legal father of any children that he would have with his brother's wife. So he refused to have sexual intercourse (with her), thereby not providing children for his brother's sake.

10   This was such an evil act in God's judgment that He also caused him to die.

11   So Yehudah said to Tamar, his (Er's) bride, "Remain a widow, and return to your father's family until my son Shelah grows up, since he thought, 'Otherwise he may die, too, just like his brothers.'" And Tamar left to return to her father's family.

12   Many days passed, then Yehudah's wife, the daughter of Shua, died. Yehudah took comfort, and along with his friend Hira the Adulamite, went to Timna to shear his sheep.

13   It was told to Tamar, "Look, your father-in-law is coming to Timna to shear his flocks."

14   She removed her widow's garments of mourning, and covered herself with a veil, sitting at the entrance to the springs on the road to Timna. She did this because Shelah had already grown up, and she had not been given to him as his wife.[6]

15   Yehudah saw her, and believed that she was a prostitute, since she had a veiled face.

---

5. v. 8: This was later known as *hoq ha-yebum* in Hebrew, the "Levirate marriage law," and is listed as a Torah commandment in Deuteronomy 25.5: "When two brothers live in the same place, and one of them dies without a son, his widow may not be sent away to marry a foreigner." (author's translation). The *yebum* (brother-in-law) will have relations with her, thereby marrying her: she will be married to him" (author's translation).

6. v. 14: Since Yehudah had not fulfilled the *hoq ha-yebum* stipulation, Tamar was going to take events into her own hands in order to have children and become once again an inheriting part of Yehudah's family.

16 So he approached her on the road, and said to her, "Let me have sexual relations with you." He did not realize that she was his daughter-in-law. She replied, "What will you give me in exchange for sexual relations?"

17 He said, "I will send you a kid from from my herd," to which she replied, "Alright, but only if you give me some collateral until you send it."

18 Then he answered, "What kind of collateral is it that I should give you?" And she said, "Your signet ring, your wrap, and your staff that is in your hand." So he gave them to her, had relations with her, and she became pregnant.

19 She then left, took off her veil, and dressed in the mourning clothes of her widowhood.

20 Yehudah sent the kid by way of his friend, the Adullamite, who was also supposed to take the collateral items back, but he could not find her (Tamar).

21 So he asked the local people, "Where is the cult prostitute who was in the roadway?" They said, "There was no cult prostitute there!"[7]

22 He then returned to Yehudah and said, "I didn't find her, and as well, the locals said that there had been no cult prostitute there."

23 Yehudah responded, "She should take possession (of the kid), or we will be shamed. After all, I sent the kid, but you didn't find her!"

24 After about three months time, Yehudah was told, "Tamar your daughter-in-law has behaved like a prostitute. She's become pregnant through her prostitution." Yehudah answered, "Bring her to judgment so that she will be burned to death."

25 So she was found and taken to her father-in-law. Then she spoke and said, "The man who owns these is the one who made me pregnant. Please, identify whose signet ring, wrap, and staff these are."[8]

---

7. *v. 21:* The use of the word *kedasha* indicates a Canaanite practice of providing cult prostitutes for ritual worship of Canaanite idols. This may bolster those who take the designation "Canaanite" in describing Tamar's family as more authentic than "merchant" (see footnote 2).

8. *v. 25:* Instead of the straight translation "bring her out," I prefer to see such a phrase as idiomatic. That is, she would be "brought out" in public in order to be found guilty of prostitution (presumably at some judgment of her elders). Thus, I prefer the translation

26 Yehudah recognized them, then answered, "She is more righteous than I am, since I did not let her marry my son Shelah." He never had sexual relations with her again.[9]

27 When her time to give birth came, she had twins in her womb.

28 As she gave birth, the midwife took a red thread and tied it to one of the baby's outstretched hands. Then she (the midwife) said, "This one (baby) was born first."

29 But as he (the baby) withdrew his hand, his brother came out instead. So she said, "What happened that you came out so fast?"And his name was called Peretz.[10]

3   Afterward, his brother who had the red thread on his hand, was born. His name was Zarach.[11]

---

that I used, which emphasizes the process that would result in her judgment, conviction, and subsequent death.

9. v. 26: Presumably this was said as a legal injunction to any death sentence, and thus was in the presence of others (Yehudah refers to her in the third person). In a section of the Talmud dealing with prudent replies, it is taught that when the narrative of Yehudah and Tamar is read, it is fit to explain the proper interpretation of the story: "(The narrative of) Tamar is to be read and interpreted. . . . What happened to Tamar and Jehudah may be read and interpreted. Is not this self-evident? Lest one say that we should care for the honor of Jehudah, they come to teach us, on the contrary, it is an honor for Jehudah that he confessed it" (Megillah 25a-b). Thus it was deemed important to explain that the outcome of the narrative shows that Yehudah was right to confess his wrongdoing. In this way, his reputation is not destroyed by his actions as recorded in this chapter. It may be that the interpretation referred to was a short translation of a biblical text from Hebrew into Aramaic during a public reading in synagogue by a *turjaman*. This was a Hebrew to Aramaic oral translator. Such translation often included a quick interpretation, similar to the one referred to in the text of Megillah. The aim was to help the public comprehend the biblical text as best as possible in Aramaic.

10. v. 29: Peretz in Hebrew means "one who breaks out," or "goes forward with power."

11. v. 30: The proper name Zarach in Hebrew means "one who rises up." The noun of this word's verbal root is used to describe the sunrise.

Chapter 39

1 So Joseph was taken down to Egypt. He was sold by the same Ishmaelites who brought him there, and was bought by Poti-far, an Egyptian who was an official of Pharaoh, and also the chief of all the cooks.[1]

2 Yet God was with Joseph, and he became successful in serving the interests of his Egyptian master.

3 His master understood that God was present with him, and that God caused him (Joseph) to succeed at everything that he did.

4 So Joseph was greatly appreciated by him. Continuing in service to him, Joseph was given responsibility for all of his business affairs. Everything was handed over to him (Joseph).

5 It was from the very moment that he put Joseph in charge of his affairs that God prospered the Egyptian's life. It was because of Joseph that the blessing of God was upon everything that he (Poti-far) owned, both at home and in his field.

6 He handed over all of his business affairs into Joseph's hands. He withheld nothing from his supervision, except for the very food that he ate. Joseph happened to be a very handsome, good-looking young man.

7 After a passage of some time, the wife of Joseph's master eyed Joseph, and said, "Have sexual relations with me."

8 But he turned her down, saying to his master's wife, "Look, my master trusts me with everything in his home. Everything that he owns has been put under my supervision.

9 No one has a more important position in this household than me. Nothing has been kept back from me, but you, since you are his wife. So how can I do such a great wrong as this, and sin against God?"

10 Yet she enticed Joseph daily, but he would not listen to her, nor sleep with her and have sexual relations with her.

---

1. *v.* 1: Presumably, the cooks for the royal family are being referred to here.

11   But one particular day, he (Joseph) entered the home to begin his work. No other household worker was present.

12   So she grabbed him by his clothes and said, "Come and have sexual relations with me." But he fled, leaving his clothes in her hands. He left and ran outside.

13   When she saw that he had left his clothes in her hands, and had run outside,[2]

14   she then screamed out to everyone in her home, and said, "Look! Did (my husband) bring this Hebrew to us so that he could treat us like fools? He just tried to rape me! That's why I screamed out loud!

15   When I screamed and shouted, he left his clothes here by me, and ran outside!"

16   She kept his clothes by her side until his (Joseph's) master arrived at home.

17   Then she told him the following story: "That Hebrew servant whom you brought here for us approached me, to violate me!

18   When I screamed in a loud voice, he left his clothes by my side, and ran off outside!"

19   His (Joseph's) master believed the words that his wife spoke to him, saying, "Your servant did such-and-such to me." So he became furious.

20   Joseph's master seized him and handed him over to the prison where the king's prisoners were kept. This prison existed for that very purpose.

21   But God was present with Joseph, and granted him great favor. The warden of the prison liked him alot.

22   So the warden put all of the inmates' affairs at that prison under Joseph's supervision. He directed all of the activities that happened there.

---

2. 2v. 13: I believe this verse hints to us that when Poti-far's wife understood the implications of what had just occurred, she was either insulted or furious at Joseph. Perhaps she had her plans to get pregnant dashed. It would have been interesting to know if she and her husband were childless, and if so she had she hoped that an affair with Joseph would make her pregnant. As a result, she came up with a fabricated story to tell her husband in case Joseph told him about what happened. In this way, she "saved face" and successfully blamed Joseph.

23 The warden did not need to oversee any of the responsibilities that he had delegated out (to Joseph), because God was with him (Joseph) to the extent that He caused everything that he did to succeed.

Chapter 40

1 After these events, the king of Egypt's drink server and his baker both committed a serious wrong against their overlord, the king of Egypt.

2 As a result, Pharaoh was livid at his two servants, the chief drink server and the chief baker.

3 So he jailed them, putting them in the cells of the chief guard, in the same prison where Joseph was imprisoned.

4 The warden put Joseph in charge of them, and he helped them. After they had been imprisoned for some time,

5 both of them had dreams during the same night. The drink server and the baker whom the king of Egypt held as prisoners had dreams that begged an interpretation.

6 Joseph came to them in the morning and saw that they were greatly disturbed.

7 So he asked Pharaoh's officials who were imprisoned with him in his overlord's prison, "Why do you look so down today?"

8 They answered him, "We've dreamed dreams and do not know how to interpret them." So Joseph said to them, "Can't God give interpretations? Please explain (your dreams) to me!"[1]

9 The chief drink server told his dream to Joseph, and said to him, "In my dream, a vine was in front of me.

10 On the vine were three twigs, and then it flowered, buds appeared, and immediately there were clusters of grapes.

11 Then Pharaoh's cup was in my hand, and I took the grapes, squeezed their juice into Pharaoh's cup, and gave the cup out of the palm of my hand to Pharaoh."

---

1. *v.* 8: In Jewish literature, Joseph is nicknamed *baal ha-chalomot* (the dreamer), based on his brothers' appellation of him in 37.19. Twice in chapter 37 (verses 5–11) and here, Joseph had dreams of great significance.

12 So Joseph told him, "This is the interpretation: the three twigs are three days.

13 In three days from now, Pharaoh will remember your situation, and return you to your position. You will give Pharaoh's cup to him, and things will return to how they used to be, when you were his drink server.

14 When this happens and matters improve for you, please remember my plight. Do a huge favor for me by mentioning me to Pharaoh, so that he will release me from prison.

15 I was kidnapped from the Land of the Hebrews, and in addition, I did not do a thing to deserve being thrown into this hole!"

16 When the chief baker learned about the good interpretation, he said to Joseph, "And I, too, in my dream saw three baskets of bread piled on my head.

17 In the top basket was a variety of Pharaoh's fine foods, but a bird ate from the basket that was on my head."

18 So Joseph answered and said, "Here is the interpretation. The three baskets are three days.

19 In three more days, Pharaoh will remember your situation, and hang you from a tree, and birds will eat the very flesh off of your skin."

20 On the third day, it was Pharaoh's birthday. So he had a banquet for all of his workers, and he remembered the situation of the chief drink server and the chief baker from among all of his servants.

21 He returned the chief drink bearer to his position, where he resumed serving drinks into Pharaoh's hands.

22 But he hung the chief baker. It ended up for them exactly as Joseph had predicted.

23 Yet the chief drink server did not remember Joseph's situation, but forgot about him.

Chapter 41

1   After two full years, Pharaoh had a dream, and he was standing by the river.

2   Seven well fed, healthy cows climbed out of the Nile, and grazed in the marsh.

3   Then seven other cows climbed out of the Nile after them, looking starved and skinny. They grazed alongside the other cows on the bank of the river.

4   The seven starving and skinny cows ate the seven well-fed, healthy cows. Then Pharaoh woke up.

5   He went back to sleep, and dreamed a second time. There were seven grain stalks growing on one reed, and they were mature and ripe.

6   Then seven more grain stalks came up after them, wilted and dried up by a *sharav*.[1]

7   The wilted, skinny stalks ate the seven mature and ripe stalks. Pharaoh woke up and knew that he had a dream.

8   In the morning he felt troubled, so he summoned all of the magicians in Egypt, and all of his wise men. Although Pharaoh explained his dream to them, none of them could interpret it for him.

9   So the chief of the royal drink servers spoke to Pharaoh, saying, "Today I remember a bad oversight of mine.

10 (When) Pharaoh was very angry with his servants, you put me under arrest in the chief guard's prison, where I was with the chief baker.

11 He and I dreamed dreams on the same night, and each of our dreams needed an interpretation.

---

1. *v. 6 and v. 23: Sharav* is modern Hebrew for a strong desert wind that blasts hot air and sand. It is also known as a *hamseen* in Arabic or a *scirocco* in Italian. This type of hot windstorm can make life difficult in the Middle East, as it fills the air with dust and sand, making breathing, seeing and eating difficult. I am surmising that the word used in our text, *qadim*, refers to the modern *sharav*.

12 A young Hebrew man who helped the chief guard was with us there. We explained our dreams to him and he interpreted each of our dreams for us.

13 Things turned out exactly according to the interpretations that he gave us. I would return to my job, but the other man would hang."

14 Pharaoh then sent for Joseph, and he was hurried out of his cell. He shaved and changed his clothes, and reported to Pharaoh.

15 Pharaoh told Joseph, "I dreamed a dream and can't interpret it. I've heard that you can listen to a dream, then interpret it."

16 So Joseph answered Pharaoh, and said, "Only God can answer Pharaoh, and give you peace."

17 Then Pharaoh told Joseph, "In my dream, I was standing on the bank of the Nile.

18 Suddenly, seven well fed and healthy cows climbed out of the Nile and grazed in the marsh.

19 Immediately, seven other cows climbed out after them. They were starved and looked skinny. No cows in all the land of Egypt looked so bad.

20 The starved and skinny cows ate the seven first, healthy ones.

21 After they had eaten, from close up it was impossible to see any difference in their appearance. It was just as bad as before.

22 I had another dream, and suddenly seven grain stalks sprouted up on one reed, full and mature.

23 Then seven wilted and shriveled grain stalks, scorched by the *sharav*, sprouted right up after them.

24 And the wilted grain stalks ate the seven mature stalks. So I told my magicians (about it), but no one could explain them to me."

25 So Joseph said to Pharaoh, "Pharaoh's dreams are about the same thing, and they will explain to Pharaoh what God is about to do.

26 The seven healthy cows represent seven years, and the seven ripe grain stalks are seven years. So, Pharaoh's dreams are about the same matter!

27 The seven starving, skinny cows that came up after the first seven years, and the seven wilted grain stalks that were burned by the *sharav*, represent a second set of seven years when there will be a famine.

28 It's just as I told Pharaoh. . . God is showing Pharaoh about what is to come!

29 So, seven years are coming that will be prosperous for the entire land of Egypt.

30 Then seven years of famine will come afterwards. It will be so harsh that providing food will be forgotten about in the land of Egypt. That's how severe the famine will be in this land.

31 Relief from hunger due to this famine will not be known in the land, because it will be very serious.

32 This dream was twice given to Pharaoh, since this message is from God, and God will make this happen soon.

33 So now Pharaoh must search for a discerning and wise man and give him authority over the affairs of the land of Egypt.

34 Pharaoh should do this and then appoint overseers over the entire land during the seven years of plenty, in order to prepare the land of Egypt.[2]

35 They should gather all types of food during the coming years of prosperity, and store grain under Pharaoh's supervision, so that there will be a supply of food kept in the cities.

36 This food will be in storage for the entire land, because of the seven years of famine that will come to Egypt. In this way, the land won't be destroyed by famine."

37 Both Pharaoh and his officials were greatly impressed by this analysis.

38 So Pharaoh told his officials, "Is there anyone like this man, who has the spirit of God in him?"[3]

2. *v.* 34: The Hebrew *chimesh* ("to prepare") can be understood as literally "arming the nation"; i.e. "equipping it" to best deal with the agronomy battle that lay ahead. This is a military term meaning "to arm." The CJB and NIV translate it as "taking a fifth (20 percent)" of all produce and storing it up to face the famine. Although I do not believe that it is the best translation, this may indeed be the *type* of action that the overseers were appointed to carry out.

3. *vv.* 38–39: It is interesting that Pharaoh seems to acknowledge the work of the One

39 Then Pharaoh said to Joseph, "Because God Himself informed you about all of these events, there is no one as discerning and wise as you!

40 You will control my royal affairs, and all my subjects will be under your authority. Only in regard to the throne will I be greater in authority than you!"

41 So Pharaoh told Joseph, "Look, I have appointed you to be over the affairs of all the land of Egypt!"

42 Then Pharaoh took his own ring off of his hand and put it on Joseph's hand. He dressed him in the best linen clothes and put a gold collar around his neck.

43 So he (Pharaoh) seated him (Joseph) in his second most important royal chariot. People cried out as he passed by, "Bow down!" The entire land of Egypt was put under his supervision.[4]

44 Pharaoh told Joseph, "I am Pharaoh! Without you, no one will make any decisions throughout the entire land of Egypt!"

45 And Pharaoh gave Joseph an (Egyptian) name: "Tsafnat-Paneach," and married him off to Osnat, the daughter of Poti-Fera, a priest from On. Joseph then traveled throughout the Land of Egypt.[5]

46 Joseph was thirty years old when he took up his position as second to Pharaoh, the king of Egypt. So Joseph was sent out by Pharaoh to inspect the entire land of Egypt.

True God in his statement. Since Pharaoh was probably an idolator, the transmission of his perspective is seen through the eyes of our historic people. In other words, Moses' scribes may be explaining to us that God caused Pharaoh to acknowledge His working through Joseph. Because of God's omniscience, these events occurred, although Pharaoh himself may not have been familiar with the God of Israel. Yet to Moses' scribes, the only viable explanation is that the Almighty was inspiring events.

4. *v.* 43: According to A.S. Yahuda, "The placement of a gold collar around the neck is a uniquely ancient Egyptian custom called the 'conferment of the Gold of Praise." Yahuda also writes about the significance of Pharaoh's ring, which he identifies as Pharaoh's signet ring. Leibel Reznick, "Egyptology in the Torah: Biblical Archaeology," 1998, http://www.aish.com/ci/sam/ 48967121.html (accessed September 6, 2009).

5. *v.* 45: *Tsafnat-Paneach* means "code-breaker" and may be the Hebrew translation of an original Egyptian name. "On" has been identified as the later city of Heliopolis, the city in the Nile Delta located a few kilometers south of modern Cairo. Throughout ancient Egyptian history, it was an important religious center and cult city, where priests such as Poti-Fera would have been employed.

47 Then the land produced abundantly for the harvests during the seven prosperous years.

48 So he (Joseph) gathered all kinds of produce during these seven years in the land of Egypt. He distributed food to the cities from the rural areas around each of them.

49 In this way, Joseph stored up so much grain that it was like the sand on the seashore. There was so much of it that they stopped trying to measure it.

50 Joseph fathered two sons prior to the onset of the years of famine. Osnat the daughter of Poti-Fera, a priest from On, bore them.

51 And Joseph named his firstborn son Menashe, because "God helped me to forget about all of my hard servitude, and all of my father's family."[6]

52 He named his second son Ephraim, because "God made me prosperous in the land of my pain and suffering."

53 Then the seven prosperous years that had been in the land of Egypt came to an end.

54 But the seven years of hunger came, just as Joseph had announced. This famine occurred in every nation. But the land of Egypt had food!

55 And then the entire land of Egypt was overtaken by famine. The people cried out to Pharaoh for food, so Pharaoh told all of Egypt: "Go to Joseph, and he will instruct you about what to do."

56 So the famine spread throughout the entire land; as a result, Joseph opened the storehouses and distributed (grain) to Egypt; yet, the famine grew stronger in the land of Egypt.

57 All the earth came into Egypt to receive grain from Joseph, because the famine was strong throughout the entire world.

---

6. *v.* 51: This could either mean that Joseph was glad to forget about his family of origin or that he missed them so much that he was crediting God with helping to ease his pain about his separation throughout his years in Egypt. The interpretation of Joseph's mindset during his upcoming family "reunion" colors how v. 51 should be taken.

Chapter 42

1 Yakov learned that there were provisions in Egypt. So he said to his sons, "Why are you hesitating?"

2 Then he told them, "Look, I've heard that there are provisions in Egypt. Go down there, and obtain food for us from there so that we can survive, and not die!"

3 So ten of Joseph's brothers went down to acquire grain from Egypt.

4 But Yakov did not send Joseph's full brother, Binyamin, along with his other brothers, as he thought, "Perhaps a tragedy may occur."

5 The sons of Yakov arrived to buy provisions along with many other people, because the famine had come to the land of Canaan.

6 And Joseph was the supervisor over the entire land, as well as the chief manager of the provisions for the entire country. Then Joseph's brothers came and prostrated themselves, face down, before him.

7 When Joseph saw his brothers, he recognized them. However, he did not reveal who he was to them, but spoke harshly to them. He asked them, "Where did you come from?," to which they answered, "From the land of Canaan, to buy food."

8 So Joseph recognized his brothers, but they did not recognize him.

9 Then Joseph remembered the dreams that he had dreamed about them. As a result, he said to them, "You are spies, and you came here to see the poverty of this land!"[1]

10 But they responded to him, saying, "No, Excellency! Your servants only came to buy food!

---

1. *v.* 9: I have translated the Hebrew word *ervah* as "poverty." In Jewish halakha, the concept of *ervah* has been developed to refer to sexual impropriety (i.e., "nakedness"; cf. Deuteronomy 24.1). Thus, the "nakedness" of the land of Egypt refers to its poverty (i.e., "nakedness," or being stripped bare of its crops). *Ervah* may also refer to strategically vulnerable places. If it does such, then Joseph was accusing his brothers of looking for a way to attack Egypt.

11 We are all the sons of one man; we are being truthful! Your servants are not spies!"

12 Yet he answered them, "No! You came to see the poverty of this land!"

13 So they responded, "We, your servants, are twelve brothers. We are the sons of one man from the land of Canaan. But the youngest is back with our father right now, and another has perished."

14 Then Joseph said to them, "It's just as I said—you are spies!

15 You will be tested by this . . . as sure as Pharaoh lives, you will not leave here until your youngest brother comes here!

16 So, one of you will be sent back to get your brother, while the rest of you will be under arrest. This is how your words will be tested, to see if you tell the truth. If not, as sure as Pharaoh lives, you are spies!"

17 Then he arrested them for three days.

18 On the third day, Joseph said to them, "Do this, and you'll live, because I fear God.

19 If you are honestly brothers, then one of you will be kept under house arrest. The rest of you, go and take grain back to your hungry families.

20 And bring your youngest brother to me. Only then will your words be believable. If you do this, then you won't die."

21 They (Joseph's brothers) said to one another, "This horrible situation has come upon us because we are guilty of harming our brother. We saw his distress, and how he begged us for mercy, but we didn't listen to him."

22 Reuven responded to them by saying: "Didn't I tell you, 'Don't do wrong to the boy,' but you didn't listen! Now we are paying for his death.'"

23 However, they didn't know that Joseph understood them, since someone was translating for them.

24 He went away from them, weeping. Then he returned to them, and spoke with them, taking Shimon away from them, placing him under house arrest right before them.

25 Joseph gave orders for their vessels to be filled with grain and to put each man's money back into his traveling bag; as well as to give them supplies for the journey. And so it was done for them.

26 They loaded their grain on their donkeys and left from there.

27 At their overnight stop, one of them opened his bag of straw to feed his donkey. He then saw his money in the lining of his traveling bag.

28 So he said to his brothers, "My money was returned! Look, in my lining!" They were all stunned, and each of them was very afraid. They said, "What has God done to us?"

29 They arrived in the land of Canaan, to their father Yakov. They told him all that had transpired to them, saying,

30 "The ruler of that land spoke very harshly with us. He figured that we were spying against his country.

31 But we told him that we are honest men, and have never been spies,

32 that we are twelve brothers, all the sons of our one father, and that the youngest was now with our father in the land of Canaan.

33 So then the man, the ruler of that land, told us: "I will only know if you are honest and the brothers of one father, when you leave (one of you) with me while you go back to your hungry families (with food).

34 And bring your youngest brother to me, so that I will know that you are not spies, but that you are honest. I will then return your brother to you, and then you may carry out your business affairs in this land."

35 When they emptied their traveling bags, each of them found a bundle of money in his bag. Each of them was petrified because of the money bundles; and their father was also very fearful.

36 Then their father Yakov said to them, "You've already deprived me of Joseph; he's no longer alive; Shimon is not with you, and now you want to take Binyamin from me? All of this so suddenly?"

37 So Reuven spoke up and said to his father: "You can put both of my sons to death if I don't personally return him (Binyamin) to you. Let me take charge of this, and I'll return him to you!"

38 But he replied, "Don't take my son with you. His brother is already dead, and he's the only one left! If something should happen to him on the road that you travel on, then I'll die in utter despair!"[2]

2. *v.* 38: Yakov thought that Binyamin was the only one of Rachel's children left alive.

Chapter 43

1   The famine was severe throughout the entire land.

2   When they finished eating all of the grain that they had brought from Egypt, their father told them: "Go back and get some more food for us."

3   So Yehudah said to him, "But that man *really* spoke strongly when he said, 'I don't want you to see me again unless your brother is with you!'

4   Only when you send our brother with us, can we go down there and get food for you!

5   But if you are not going to send (him), we won't go back there, because that man said to us, 'I don't want you to see me again unless your brother is with you!'"

6   So Israel answered, "Why have you done this rotten thing to me by telling that man that you have another brother?"

7   Then they answered, "Because he insisted on asking us where our homeland was and asked us directly, 'Is your father living? Do you have a brother?' So we answered him according to the questions! How could we know that he would tell us to bring our brother down?"

8   Again, Yehudah spoke to Israel his father: "Send the boy with me; we'll go together; that way we, you, and our children will all live and not die.

9   I guarantee his protection, and you can blame me if I don't bring him back to you. You can hold me responsible for the rest of my life.

10 If we hadn't dilly-dallied for so long, we'd already be there and back by now."

11 So their father, Israel, said, "If that's the case, then do this: take some balsam, honey, fragrant resin, myrrh, nuts and almonds from the best delicacies of the Land; put them in your vessels and take them to that man as a gift.

12 Also, take twice as much silver along with you as was in the lining of your traveling bags, to return it. Maybe it was all a mistake.

13 And take your brothers along; go and return to that man.

14 And may God Almighty show you mercy with that man, so that he'll send back your brother Binyamin. Should I become bereaved, then I guess I'll become bereaved.'"

15 So the men gathered their gift, took twice the amount of silver, and along with Binyamin, went down to Egypt, then stood before Joseph.

16 Joseph saw that Binyamin was with them, so he said to his chief household servant: "Bring these men home and slaughter meat, then prepare it, because these men will be eating with me at noon."

17 The servant did exactly what Joseph had instructed him. He brought the men to Joseph's home.

18 Because the men were brought to Joseph's home, they were fearful. They said to each other, "It's because of the money that must be returned from our traveling bags from the first time. We are being taken in order to be stripped of our possessions. We will be attacked, and taken captive as slaves, and our donkeys will be seized."

19 They came up to Joseph's chief servant at the entry to the home, and spoke to him.

20 "Please, sir," they said, "We really *did* come down the first time to buy food.

21 It was when we came to our resting place for the night that we opened our traveling bags, and suddenly there was money in each of our bag linings. Each of us has now returned this exact amount!

22 There was other money that we brought in our own hands with which to buy food. So we don't know *who* put the money into our traveling bags!"

23 But he responded, "Peace be to you! Don't fear. Your God, the God of your fathers, gave you the treasure in your traveling bags. It was *me* who passed on this money." Then he brought out Shimon to them.[1]

---

1. *v.* 23: There are two possibilities as to the action that Joseph's servant took. One is that he "passed this money on", meaning that he is the one, who on Joseph's orders, put

24 So the man brought them to Joseph's home, gave them water, and washed their feet. Then he gave straw to their donkeys.

25 They prepared the gift for Joseph's arrival at noon, since they heard that they would eat a meal there.

26 When Joseph came home, they brought him the gift that they had taken to his house. They prostrated themselves to the ground to honor him.

27 So he asked them how they were, and afterward said to them: "How is your elderly father, whom you told me was still living?"

28 They responded: "Your servant, our father, is alive and well." And they bowed down and prostrated themselves before him.

29 He looked over to see his full brother Binyamin, and then said: "Is this your youngest brother that you told me about?" And he (Joseph) said to him (Binyamin), "May God be good to you, my son."

30 Immediately, Joseph hurried away because he felt highly emotional about seeing his brother. He looked for a place to cry and went to another room and wept there.

31 Afterwards, he washed his face. When he was able to control himself, he came out, and said: "Serve the food."

32 Joseph and his brothers were then served separately, away from each other. The Egyptians who ate with him were also seated by themselves. This is because Egyptians would not eat with Hebrews, because the Egyptians considered them vile. [2]

---

the money into the linings of the traveling bags. This may be what he is trying to tell the brothers. Or, perhaps the text is telling us that this servant had received all of the money that was in the traveling bags that the brothers had given back to him, thus their "debt" was paid. They would not be considered thieves, and they shouldn't be concerned anymore about this matter. I have translated the text to mean the former. 44.1, however, may argue for the latter interpretation.

    2. *v.* 32: The Targum, in its translation, gives interesting insight as to why this was the case. It states: "Then they set it out for him by himself, and for them by themselves, and for the Egyptians who were eating with him by themselves, for the Egyptians are not able to eat food with the Hebrews, because the livestock that the Egyptians worship, the Hebrews eat" (Clem translation).

33 Later, they sat in front of him in order, the eldest (brother) to the youngest. Each of them (the brothers) was amazed (at the situation they were in).

34 By his authority, the food was dished out to them, and Binyamin's servings were five handfuls more (than anyone else's). So they drank, imbibing together with him.[3]

---

3. *v.* 34: The Masoretic text is clear that the men all drank a fermented drink in stating *vayishtakru 'ito*. Beer was a very common beverage in ancient Egypt, and it could very well be that this is what they were drinking in our verse. See Caroline Seawright, "Ancient Egyptian Alcohol," *Caroline Seawright's Egyptology Column*, March 12, 2001, http://www .thekeep.org/~kunoichi/   kunoichi/themestream/egypt_alcohol.html   (accessed September 6, 2009) and Brian Madigan, "Ancient Egyptian Bread Making," *EMuseum at Minnesota State University Mankato* 2002, http://www.mnsu.edu/emuseum/prehistory/egypt/dailylife/breadmaking.htm (accessed September 6, 2009). Although in *v.* 34 I translated the text to mean that Binyamin received "five handfuls" more than his other brothers, the phrase *chamesh yadot* (literally "five hands") may mean five measures; that is, five times what his brothers received, no matter what standard of measure was used. Although there is a word in modern Hebrew to literally describe "a handful" (*chofen*), it is not certain that this word was in use during the age of the biblical patriarchs.

Chapter 44

1   He instructed his chief household servant, "Fill the traveling bags of these men with as much food as they can carry, and put money in each of their bag linings.

2   And put my silver cup in the lining of the youngest one, along with money for buying his food." He did exactly what Joseph instructed.

3   When morning broke, the men were sent away, along with their donkeys.

4   They left the city and weren't far away when he said to his chief household servant, "Go, follow these men, and catch up to them. Then ask them, 'Why have you paid back good with evil?

5   Isn't this the cup out of which my master drinks? Doesn't he use it to discern (your character)? You have acted with evil intent!'"[1]

6   So he caught up to them, and said those very words.

7   But they responded to him, saying: "Why would my master say such things as these? God forbid that your servants would do such a thing!

8   We already returned the money to you that we found in the lining of our bags in the land of Canaan. So why would we steal either money or gold from the home of your master?

9   If this can be found among any of your servants, let him die. Then we who remain will become slaves to my master!"

---

1. *v.* 5: The Hebrew verb, *le'nachesh* can be "to divine"; that is, to predict the future, referring to an Egyptian occult practice. However, my translation is conjecturing that Joseph meant to test *his brothers* through the incident of the "stolen" cup. Perhaps he wanted to see how his brothers would behave, and if any of them would come to the aid of Binyamin, the seeming thief in this incident. The cup of "divination," then, is more of a "cup of discernment of character" and is directly tied to the behavior of the brothers rather than to Egyptian occult practice. On the other hand, the timing and flow of the text could argue for the more common translation, "cup of divination." But the way in which Joseph *actually uses* the cup in relation to his overall plan of action in this chapter argues for my translation.

10 So he responded, "Let it be as you say. However, the one who has it will be my servant, and the rest of you will be innocent."

11 They then hurried: each one brought his bag to the ground and opened his bag.

12 He (the servant) carefully searched, starting with the youngest one, and the cup was found in Binyamin's bag.

13 So they (the brothers) tore their cloaks. They each loaded up their donkeys and started back toward the city.

14 Yehudah and his brothers arrived at Joseph's home. He was still there, so all of them prostrated themselves on their faces.

15 Then Joseph asked them, "What is this that you have done? Didn't you know that a man like me has the ability to test your characters?"

16 So Yehudah said, "What can we say to your Excellency? What can we possibly say? What can justify us? God has paid us back for our sin. So, we are your servants, my master—all of us, including the one who had the cup with him."

17 He then responded: "God forbid that I would do such a thing. The one who was found with the cup in his possession will be my servant. The rest of you can go home in peace to your father."

18 But Yehudah approached him, and said: "I beg of you, Excellency, let your servant speak a few words to my master, and please don't get angry at your servant, because you are as Pharaoh himself.

19 My master asked his servant, 'Do you have a father or a brother?'

20 And we answered my master: 'We have an elderly father, and his youngest son, fathered in his old age. His full brother has already died, and he remains the only son of his mother. His father absolutely adores him.'

21 So you said to your servants: 'Bring him down to me, so I can see him.'

22 We then told my master, 'The boy can't leave his father. If he leaves, his father would die!'

23 So you said to your servants, 'If your youngest brother doesn't come down with you, you won't see me again.'

24 When we went back to your servant my father, we relayed to him the words of my master.

25 Our father responded by saying, 'Return and get some food for us.'

26 So we said, 'We won't go down unless our youngest brother is with us, because we can't see the man if our youngest brother is not with us.'

27 Your servant my father said to us, 'You know that my wife bore me two (sons).[2]

28 One of them left me, and I haven't seen him till this very day. So I concluded, 'He was torn to pieces.'

29 Now if you take the other son away from me and some tragedy occurs, you'll send me to my death in agony.'

30 If I return to your servant my father, and the boy isn't with us, because their lives are so emotionally connected with each other,

31 when he sees that the boy isn't there, he will die. Your servants will then have made your servant our father go to the grave in agony.'

32 But your servant guaranteed the life of the boy to my father. I said: 'If I don't bring him back to you, I will be responsible to my father for the rest of my life.'

33 Please now, let your servant take the place of the boy, to become my master's servant, so that the boy can go back up to his father.[3]

2. *vv.* 21, 23, 24, 27, 30 *and* 32: The adjective "your servant" is an ancient expression that is still used in the Middle East today. When someone is introduced to another, he may be introduced in Arabic as *Yusuf abduka* (Joseph, your servant). That is, the pattern is one's proper name followed by *abduka* (your servant). In Hebrew this is more archaic-sounding, and although it may happen in a given situation, it is not a part of modern colloquial Hebrew.

3. *v.* 33: The Hebrew verb *le'alot* ("go back up") shows a geographic bent. The Land of Israel is seen as the place of spiritual depth and meaning, as it is the scene of biblical events and because of the promises in the Torah concerning the Jewish people in the Land of Israel. Thus, it is "elevated" above all lands, and one "goes up" to Israel (that is, "arrives in, immigrates or moves to" the Land). Geographically, the land itself rises in elevation from the Mediterranean coast to the city of Jerusalem, considered the most holy city of the land. Thus within Israel, one "goes up" to Jerusalem. Always, it is the spiritual ideal to both ascend geographically higher to the holy city, while improving one's relationship

34 Otherwise, how can I return to my father without the boy along with me? I would then see horrible sorrows befall my father."

---

with the God of Israel. So when the text describes Jacob's sons as "going up" from Egypt to Israel, this ideal is relayed through the language. With this ideal, as people come to Israel, and study and practice Torah, one's spirituality is affected positively (also see 45.25 and 46.4 for similar uses of this word). One has "gone up" both geographically and hopefully, in a spiritual manner. Conversely, the text describes Jacob's family as literally "going down" or descending from the Land to other nations (here, Egypt) through the use of the verb le'redet (cf. 44.23, 45.9, 45.13, 46.3 and in 46.4 where it is used to describe God going "down" to Egypt with Yakov!)

Chapter 45

1   At that point, Joseph could no longer control his emotions, so he had all the servants who were present leave. No one was there with him, so Joseph revealed who he was to his brothers.

2   He began to weep loudly, so that the Egyptians as well as Pharaoh's family heard him.[1]

3   Then Joseph said to his brothers, "I am Joseph! Is my father still living?" His brothers could not talk because they were so shocked!

4   So Joseph told his brothers: "Please come here to me", and they came. He said, "I am Joseph your brother, whom you sold into Egypt!

5   But now, don't be distraught and don't be mad at yourselves because you sold me. Look, it was to preserve life that God sent me ahead of you,

6   because there have now been two years of famine in the heartland of this country, and there are another five years to go with no sower or reaper.

7   God sent me ahead of you, so that your family would remain alive in this land, and to provide a great refuge for you.

8   Now, it wasn't you who sent me here, but God. He has made me a father figure to Pharaoh and the supervisor over his entire royal house, the governor of all the land of Egypt.

9   Hurry, go up to my father and tell him: 'Your son Joseph says, 'God has made me the master of all Egypt. Come down to me. Don't delay!

---

1. This could mean that either the Egyptian servants whom he had sent out heard him weep with their own ears, or that, generally speaking, the Egyptian people all the way up to Pharaoh's royal court heard *about this event* (thus, *va'yishma bet pharaoh* in the text here would mean "Pharaoh's royal court heard *about* the incident," as we have in 45.16). Most commentators, including this one, assume that Joseph began to speak in Hebrew to his brothers, thus revealing who he was to them. A fascinating article on this subject is Gad Sarfatti, "Did the Patriarchs Speak Hebrew?" www.biu.ac.il/JH/Parasha/eng/vayigash/vayigash.shtml.

10 You (Yakov) can live in the area of Goshen, and be close to me—you, your sons, and your grandchildren; your flocks and cattle, and all that you have!

11 I will provide for you there, because there is five more years of famine; this way you, your sons and all that you have won't be in dire need.

12 Then you will see, and my brother Binyamin will see that it is I who speak with both of you!

13 So tell my father about the high honor that I have in Egypt, and about everything that you have seen! Hurry up, and come back down with here with my father!"

14 He embraced Binyamin his brother, and Binyamin cried in his arms.

15 Then he embraced and kissed each of his brothers, and he wept over them. After this, his brothers were able to speak with him.

16 Pharaoh's royal court heard about this incident, and said: "Joseph's brothers arrived." Pharaoh felt favorable about what had happened, and so did all of his servants.

17 So Pharaoh instructed Joseph, saying: "Tell your brothers, do this: load up your donkeys, and go back to the land of Canaan.

18 Then take your father and your households and come to me. I will give you the best part of the land of Egypt, and you will eat from the best food of the land.

19 So now, you've also been instructed to do this: take carts from the land of Egypt for your children and wives, and they will carry your father, and return!

20 You won't need to be concerned about how full your vessels are, because the best of all the land of Egypt is yours."

21 So Israel's sons did exactly that, and Joseph gave them carts just as Pharaoh ordered. He also gave them supplies for their journey.

22 Each man was given a change of garments, and in addition Binyamin was given 300 pieces of silver, along with five changes of garments.

23 He sent the following for his father: ten donkeys carrying the best produce of Egypt and ten mules carrying grain, bread, and food items for
his father for the journey back (to Egypt).

24 So he sent his brothers, and they left. He said to them: "Don't get angry
with each other while on the road!"[2]

25 They went up out of Egypt and came to their father Yakov in the land
of Canaan.

26 It was then that they told him, "Joseph is still alive! He is the ruler over
all the land of Egypt!" As a result, he fainted; he did not believe them.

27 But they told him all the words that Joseph instructed them to say. He
saw the carts that Joseph had sent to carry him, and then Yakov their
father revived and felt more alert.

28 Then Israel said, "What a tremendous surprise that my son is still alive!
I must go down to see him before I die!"[3]

2. *v.* 24: I surmise that Joseph was concerned that his siblings might quarrel on the
way home, either about who was guilty for Joseph's disappearance, as they had done
previously (cf. 42.21–22), or that he was trying to prevent anyone from being envious
of the favors that Binyamin had just received. Joseph certainly wanted the return trip to
Israel to be completed quickly and successfully.

3. Of course, Israel meant these words in a very positive vein! An alternative translation could be, "What wonderful news—my son is still alive!" Only one Hebrew word
(*rav*) is used to express Israel's reaction to this great news. This word has an array of
possible meanings, all pointing to this news as being great and wonderful. One can only
imagine the emotional force that this must have had to Yakov—and thus we see him
called Israel in the text (which again signifies that he is a fulfilled person, and is reaching
his destiny).

Chapter 46

1   So Israel traveled with all of his possessions, arriving at Beersheva. He sacrificed offerings to the God of his father, Isaac.[1]

2   Then God spoke to Israel in a vision during the night, saying: "Yakov, Yakov!" He responded, "I'm already here!"[2]

3   So He said: "I am God, the God of your fathers! Don't be afraid of going down to Egypt, because it is there that I will make you a great people.

4   I will go down with you to Egypt and I will definitely bring you up back up! And Joseph will be present with you when you die."

---

1. *v*.1 It is quite interesting that the text twice refers to Yakov as "Israel," (45.28 and here) before reverting back to the name Yakov in v. 2. This leads to a quick conclusion that the use of the name "Israel" is purposeful. Perhaps it denotes a happy, fulfilled and victorious man. Dr. Amos Bar-da of Bar Ilan University has commented on this in saying: "The life of the father of the nation fluctuates along the scale from Jacob (Yakov) to Israel; between the earthly and the divine." See "Making the Crooked Straight," Parashat Va-Yetze 5768, *Bar-Ilan University's Parashat Hashavua Study Center*, November 17, 2008, http://www.biu.ac.il/JH/Parasha/eng/ vayetze/amo.html (accessed September 6, 2009). Bar-da sees a difference in the use of these two names, as well. When the name "Yakov" is used, I believe that something less than a fulfilled, satisfied patriarch is presented, whereas the use of "Israel" implies a man who sees his destiny fulfilled.

2. *v.* 2: I have translated the Hebrew word *hineni* to show the enthusiastic reply that this response entailed. It does mean "here I am," as it is often translated. However, in the context of this momentous event in Yakov's life, I translated it with a strong, joyful response. Isaiah expresses this exact same idiomatic usage of this word in Isaiah 6.8: "And I heard the voice of the Almighty, saying, 'Who will I send, and who will go out for us?' So I said, '*I'm already here!* Send me!'" (author's translation). It is as if Isaiah is waving his hand in front of God like a pupil who can't wait to be called upon to answer his teacher's question. Even though these events happened in visions to both Isaiah and Yakov, I can't picture that either of them would have wanted anyone else to answer God's summons to them. Another use of this same word is found in Bereshit 22.1, where it is written, "It was after these events that God made Avraham pass through a great ordeal. So He said to him, 'Avraham.' He (Avraham) replied, '*I'm right here!*'" (italics and translation mine). My rendering of *hineni* in this verse as 'I'm right here' expresses a similar tone as in my other translations of *hineni*; i.e., 'I'm already here.' There is enthusiasm and desire expressed in all of these responses.

5   Yakov rose up and left Beersheva. Israel's sons took Yakov their father, their children, and their wives in the carts that Pharaoh had sent to bring them.

6   They also took their cattle and their possessions that they had acquired in the land of Canaan. So Yakov and all of his clan came with him into Egypt.

7   His grandsons were with him, along with his daughters and grand-daughters. All of his descendants came with him into Egypt.

8   These are the names of Israel's sons who came into Egypt: Yakov and his sons: Reuven, Yakov's firstborn;

9   Reuven's sons were Hanoch, Falu, Chetzron, and Carmi. Shimon's sons were Yemuel, Yamin, Ohad, Yachin, Sohar, and Shaul, the son of a Canaanite woman.

10 Levi's sons were Gershon, Kehat, and Merari.

11 Yehudah's sons were Er, Onan, Shelah, Peretz, and Zarach.

12 But Er and Onan died in the land of Canaan. Peretz' sons were Chetzron and Chamul.

13 Yissachar's sons were Tola, Fuvah, Yov and Shimron.

14 Zevulun's sons were Sered, Elon and Yachelel.

15 These are Leah's sons that she bore to Yakov in Padan Aram. There was also her daughter, Dinah. All of his sons and daughters (through Leah) numbered thirty-three.

16 Gad's sons are Sifyon, Hagai, Shuni, Etzbon, Eri, Arodi, and Areli.

17 Asher's sons are Yimnah, Yishvah, Yishvi, Veriah, Serach, and Achotam. Veriah's sons were Chever and Malkiel.

18 These are the sons of Zilpah (whom Lavan gave to his daugher Leah). She gave birth to sixteen persons in Yakov's clan.

19 Yakov's wife Rachel gave birth to two sons, Joseph and Binyamin.

20 Joseph's sons Menashe and Efrayim were born to him in the land of Egypt by Osnat, the daughter of Poti-Fera, a priest of On.

21 Binyamin's sons are Bela, Vecher, Ashbel, Gera, Na'aman, Achi, Rosh, Muppim, Chuppim, and Ared.

22 These are Rachel's sons that she bore for Yakov. They were fourteen in number.

23 Dan's son was Chushim.

24 Naftali's sons were Yachse'el, Guni, Yetzer, and Shilem.

25 These are the sons of Bilhah (whom Lavan gave to Rachel, his daughter). She gave birth to seven people in Yakov's clan.

26 Everyone who came with Yakov into Egypt was his offspring, except for the wives of Yakov's sons. Their entire number was sixty-six people.

27 Also, Joseph's sons who were born in Egypt were two in number. Yakov's family who came to Egypt numbered, in total, seventy persons.

28 He (Yakov) sent Yehudah in front of him to find Joseph, to get directions for entering Goshen. Finally he arrived in the land of Goshen!

29 Then Joseph got his chariot ready and went up to meet his father Israel in Goshen. When he saw him, he embraced him, and cried and cried in his embrace.[3]

30 So Israel said to Joseph, "Now I am ready to die, because I've seen you and you are still alive!"

31 Then Joseph spoke to his brothers and to his father's family: "I will go and speak to Pharaoh. I'll tell him that my brothers and my father's family from the land of Canaan have come to me.

---

3. *vv.* 29–30: Yakov is "Israel" in these two verses. This usage again brings up the possibility that "Israel" is used when Yakov is portrayed as a happy, fulfilled and victorious man, as the name *Israel* connotes (it means "prince with God," or "one who struggles with God, or on behalf of God" [and wins]). An interesting article on this very subject states: "The dual name 'Yaakov-Yisrael' reflects two aspects of Yaakov's life. . . .The name 'Yaakov' is synonymous with all the difficulties he would endure while dealing with his brother. When Yaakov was victorious in his fight with the angel, who . . . (the rabbis) interpret to be the Angel of Esav, Yaakov was given a new name, 'Yisrael,' meaning, one who has overcome his foes. There are times when he was victorious and as such referred to as 'Yisrael,' yet he endured many hardships, and was constantly reminded that he was also 'Yaakov.'" Zvi Sobolofsky, "Yakov and Israel, A Dual Destiny," 1999, http://www.torahweb.org/torah/1999/parsha/rsob_vayishlach.html (Accessed September 6, 2009).

32 And that they are shepherds and cattle herders; they have brought their flocks and cattle, along with all that they have.

33 So when Pharaoh summons you and asks, 'What is your profession?'

34 then say, 'Your servants are cattle herders from our youth till now: both we and our ancestors before us.' Because of this, you must live in the land of Goshen because Egyptians dislike all shepherds."[4]

---

4. *v.* 34: Working with cattle and flocks was considered "beneath" the dignity of Pharaoh's royal house. See 43.32 and the commentary to it.

Chapter 47

1   So Joseph approached Pharaoh and told him, "My father, my brothers, their flocks, cattle and all of their possessions have arrived from the land of Canaan, and are now in the land of Goshen."

2   He took five of his brothers and introduced them to Pharaoh.

3   Then Pharaoh said to his brothers: "What is your profession?" So they responded to Pharaoh, "Your servants are shepherds; we and our ancestors before us."

4   They then answered Pharaoh by saying, "We came to live in this land, because there is no pasture land for your servants' flocks. The famine is very severe in the land of Canaan. So please allow your servants to live in the land of Goshen."

5   Pharaoh then spoke to Joseph: "Your father and your brothers have come to you.

6   All the land of Egypt is yours; you may settle your father and brothers in the best part of the land. They may live in the area of Goshen. If you know of any of them who are outstanding, make them officials who are in charge of my own cattle."

7   Finally, Joseph brought his father Yakov to meet Pharaoh, and Yakov gave Pharaoh a blessing.

8   Then Pharaoh said to Yakov, "How old are you?"

9   Yakov responded to Pharaoh: "My days on earth have been 130 years; my time has been short and extremely hard. I'm not as old as my ancestors were."

10 So Yakov pronounced a blessing for Pharaoh, then left his presence.

11 Then Joseph settled his father and his brothers by giving them a permanent land holding in the land of Egypt. It was in the best of that area, in the land of Ramses, just as Pharaoh had instructed.

12 And Joseph supported his father and his brothers, as well as his father's entire clan with food, according to the number of children.

13 There was no food in the entire land, as the famine was very severe. Both the land of Egypt and the land of Canaan were made destitute by the famine.

14 Joseph then took all the money that was found in the land of Egypt and in the land of Canaan with which people paid for food. Joseph brought the money to Pharaoh's royal court.

15 All monetary transactions had ceased in the land of Egypt and in the land of Canaan. Then all of Egypt came to Joseph, saying, "Bring us food; why should we die just because we have no money?"

16 Then Joseph answered: "If you have no money, bring your cattle, and I'll give you (food) in exchange for your cattle."

17 So they brought their cattle to Joseph, and Joseph gave them food in exchange for their horses and cattle, their sheep and cows, and their donkeys. He managed to get through that year by exchanging food for cattle.

18 That year ended, and they again came to him during the next year, saying to him, "We can't keep our situation hidden from our Excellency— because our money and livestock belong to our Excellency, we have nothing left in our Excellency's sight but our bodies and our land.

19 Why should we die and you do nothing? Buy both us and our land in exchange for food. Then both we and our land will be in service to Pharaoh. And then give us seeds so that we can live and not die! Only then will the land not become wasteland."

20 So Joseph bought up all the farmland in Egypt for Pharaoh.[1]

21 Every single Egyptian sold his field since the famine was so harsh on them. Then the land (legally) became Pharaoh's. Then he moved people from one city to another, and from one end of the border of Egypt to the other.

22 But he did not buy up the land of the priests, because the provisions for the priests came directly from Pharaoh himself. They ate what Pharaoh himself daily provided for them, and so there was no need to sell their land.

---

1. *v.* 20: Pharaoh was already in political control over the entire land of Egypt, so it is the legal ownership of the physical land that is being talked about here. The severity of the famine ended private ownership of the land, and "nationalized" the farmland.

23 Then Joseph declared to the people: "Look, I bought you and your land today for Pharaoh. Here are seeds so you can sow the land.

24 When the crops are ready, you will give a fifth to Pharaoh, and keep four parts by which you will both seed the fields and eat; it is for your families and children to eat."

25 They responded: "You have renewed our lives! Your Excellency has done a great favor for us. We are now the servants of Pharaoh!"

26 Joseph made it a law till this very day concerning the physical ground of Egypt: one fifth (of the crops) belong to Pharaoh, with the exception of the priests' land, where Pharaoh would not possess anything.

27 Israel lived in the region of Goshen in the land of Egypt. They settled it, were fruitful and had many children.

28 Yakov lived in the land of Egypt for seventeen years. He was 147 years old.

29 Israel came to the end of his life, so he called for his son Joseph, and said to him, "If you could please do me a favor, put your hand under my thigh, and perform for me an act of kindness and truth: please do not bury me in Egypt.[2]

30 But I shall be buried with my fathers, and you will carry me from Egypt and bury me in their burial cave." So he answered: "I will certainly do as you wish."[3]

31 So he (Yakov) said: "Swear this to me by an oath"; so he made an oath to him. Then Israel prostrated himself on the head of his bed.[4]

---

2. *v.* 29: Putting one's hand under someone's thigh symbolized the act of pledging or giving an oath to perform a deed on their behalf. In particular, this was done for persons who were dying, as one today might express in words their last dying wish for family members to perform.

3. *v.* 30: To understand the full import of this request, see Moshe Lichtmann, "Do Not Bury Me in Egypt," http://www.torahmitzion.org/pub/parsha/5768/vayechi.pdf. If Joseph was asking to be buried in the Macpelah Cave ('in their burial cave'), then it is interesting to note that he was buried in Shechem instead, and not at Macpelah (located outside Hevron); however, his burial was in the Land of Israel and in the tribal inheritance of Ephraim, the son of Joseph.

4. *v.* 31: The reader is advised to study the entire subject of oath-making and oath-taking as developed in Jewish jurisprudence. Tractate Shevuot of the Talmud is fit for reference material on this subject (along with a good teacher).

Chapter 48

1   After these events, Joseph was told, "Look, your father is ill." So he took his two sons, Menashe and Ephraim, with him.

2   It was told to Yakov, "Here, your son Joseph is coming to be with you." Then Israel felt stronger, and sat up in bed.[1]

3   Yakov told Joseph, "God Almighty appeared to me in Luz in the land of Canaan, and He blessed me.

4   And He said to me, "Now I will make you fruitful and will make you numerous. Therefore I will cause you to be a nation of unified tribes. So I have given this Land as an everlasting possession to your future descendants.

5   Now, your two sons who were born to you in the land of Egypt, up to the time of my arrival in Egypt, they are mine; Ephraim will be to me like Reuven and Shimon.[2]

6   But your children who will be born after them will be yours, and they will inherit along with their own brothers.

---

1. *v. 2:* The text can be telling us that Yakov either sat upon the bed, or that he sat up while still lying in bed. I have translated the verse according to the latter alternative.

2. *v. 5:* By stating his 'claim' of possession regarding Ephraim and Menashe, I believe that Yakov legally adopted the two sons of Joseph here. In this Torah portion, we also read about the adoption of Joseph's sons, Ephraim and Manasseh, by their grandfather, Jacob. At first, Jacob states that Ephraim and Manasseh will be to him like his own sons (Genesis 48.5). Then further on, we read of the biblical practice of placing the adoptee on the new parent's knees (Genesis 48.12). Jacob's adoption of his grandsons is not a new concept in the Torah; in fact, adoption is mentioned numerous times in Genesis. It is as if the boys are pictured to have come from Yakov's conjugal act with *his* wife, instead of from Joseph. Yakov's statement equivocated Ephraim and Menasseh with Reuven and Shimon; thus Yakov gave them the same family status as his two firstborn sons. The content of verse 6 also strengthens this reading of the text. We can ask why this was necessary. To some degree, the Egyptian background of Joseph's sons, coupled with their birth to an Egyptian mother whose father was a pagan priest, necessitated legal adoption. To have the legal status so that they could be inheritors both of the covenant promises given to their grandfather and of the family blessings, they had to be "put back" as it were, into the family. Adoption would do such.

7   When I arrived from Padan, Rachel died in the land of Canaan, on the road, at some distance from the entrance to Efrat. So I buried her there on the road. Efrat is Bet-Lechem."

8   Then Israel saw the sons of Joseph, and said, "Who are they?"

9   So Joseph said to his father, "They are my sons whom God gave me." And he (Yakov) replied, "Please bring them to me so that I can bless them."

10   Israel's eyes were weak from old age, and he was unable to see well. So he (Joseph) brought them to him, and he kissed and hugged them.

11   Then Israel said to Joseph, "I didn't think that I'd ever see you again, and now God has even let me see your offspring."

12   Joseph removed them from between his (Yakov's) knees, then prostrated himself in worship to God.

13   So Joseph took both of them, placing Ephraim on his right (thus on Israel's left), and Menashe on his left (thus on Israel's right). Then he (Joseph) approached him (Israel).

14   Israel reached out his right hand and put it on the head of Ephraim, the younger son; his left hand was put purposely on the head of Menashe, even though Menashe was the first-born son.

15   He then blessed Joseph, saying, "May God, before Whom my fathers Avraham and Isaac lived righteously, the God Who has shepherded me from far back until today,

16   and may the messenger-angel who redeemed me from all evil give the boys a reason to bend their knees in thanksgiving. They will be called by my name, as well as the name of my fathers Avraham and Isaac. So will they spread out in great numbers in the midst of the Land.[3]

---

3. v.16: The phrase "called by my name" may be a confirmation of the adoption that just took place. Ephraim and Menashe are now legally in Yakov's family, and therefore can be called "by my name," that is, "sons of Israel," as our Torah text in short order calls their offspring. A further meaning may be connected by expanding the meaning of the word *shem* (name) in Hebrew. Though *shem* usually means a name, it can also refer to *a persons reputation*; e.g., both the phrase and the proper name *shem*-tov in modern Hebrew means "a person with a good reputation." Perhaps the text tells us that Yakov's heritage and history was to be inherited by Ephraim and Menashe, as well.

17 When Joseph saw that his father placed his right hand on Ephraim's head, it bothered him greatly. He tried to guide his father's hand by removing it from on top of Ephraim's head.

18 So Joseph told his father, "Not like that, my father! Since this one (Menashe) is the first born, put your hand on his head!"

19 However, his father would not budge, saying, "I know, my son, I know. He also will be a tribe that will be great. But his younger brother will be greater than him. His descendants will be a prominent tribe."[4]

20 Then he (Yakov) blessed them on that day, saying, "Through you, Israel will bestow blessings, by saying, 'May God make you like Ephraim and Menashe'", and he put Ephraim before Menashe.

21 So Israel told Joseph, "Look, I am ready to die; may God be with all of you, and bring you back to the Land of your fathers.

22 And I have given to you the area of Shechem, which I took from the Emorites with my sword and bow."

---

4. *v.* 19: The ending Hebrew phrase to this verse is *melo hagoyim* (I translated this as "prominent among the tribes"). This refers to the half-tribe of Ephraim being a very strong tribe with a vibrant lifestyle and economy that makes it outstanding in Israel. In history, the half-tribe of Ephraim became synonymous with the Northern Kingdom of Israel (cf. Jeremiah 31.8, 31.19, 51.19, Hosea 5 [repeatedly], Zechariah 9.13). Ephraim's tribal land holdings made it the center of the kingdom. Perhaps this type of prominence is being referred to in this verse.

Another possible translation is "the best of the nations," and may refer to the quality of society, lifestyle or families. If simple size is being referred to, then "teeming with people" may be a good descriptive translation. Following that line of thought, Yakov is foretelling that Ephraim will be a large tribe in terms of the numbers of its people. In Numbers 2.18–19, during the time of Israel's travels in the Sinai peninsula, the text reads: "The flag of the camp of Ephraim and its army will be toward the west. The chief official of the tribe of Ephraim is Elishama ben Amihud. Its division has 40,500 people." We are then informed that the half-tribe of Menashe and the tribe of Binyamin will march under the leadership of the tribe of Ephraim: "All the people of the camp of Ephraim were 108,100. They marched as the third division" (Numbers 2.24). We see some role of prominence given here to Ephraim, though the tribe's numbers are not incredibly larger than the other tribes. Their flag was the prominent one in this division of three tribes. So, Yakov's words may be partially fulfilled here as relayed by these facts, however not in any pompous nor exaggerated way.

Chapter 49

1 So Yakov called for his sons and said, "Gather around, and I will explain to you what will happen to you at the end of history.[1]

2 Gather around, and listen, Jacob's sons! Pay attention to Israel, your father![2]

3 Reuven is my firstborn. You are the proof of my strength and early manhood, full of honor and full of might,

4 but running like water; you won't be special, because you climbed into your father's bed, and defiled my couch by getting into it.

5 Shimon and Levi, 'the brothers'; their blades are tools of wanton violence.

6 I will not join them in their secrets; my conscience will not allow me to take part in their actions, because in their fiery anger they killed a man. They wanted to neuter a bull![3]

7 Cursed are their tempers; their anger is strong and unbridled. So I will divide them in Yakov, and scatter them in Israel.[4]

1. *v.1:* This particular Hebrew term that I translated as "the end of history" (Hebrew, *acharit hayamim*) is most often used to denote the ending time period of human history. It is used as such in the Torah's prophetic writings. Some commentators attribute this era to be the Messianic era (in Hebrew, *chevlay hamashiach*). I refer the reader to Tractate Sanhedrin, pages 98a–99b for the Jewish sages' discussion of this time period.

2. *v. 2:* The names "Yakov" and "Israel" are often used interchangeably in the same chapter. However, it is my observation that when "Israel" is used, the Torah is drawing our attention to his identification as the chosen man of God, whose descendants will inherit the Land. The name is perhaps a simple reminder of the fact that this is the same Yakov who the inheritor of the Land, and the covenant promises.

3. *v. 6:* To "neuter a bull" was probably an ancient Hebrew saying or idiomatic phrase, meaning that they destroyed the men of a city (the men of Shechem, to be exact). This may be a way to say "flay a bull." Perhaps the rite of circumcision is likened here to neutering a bull. If the idiom means to flay a bull instead of neutering it, the picture is even more graphic.

4. *v. 7:* By "in Yakov," it is meant that these two sons will not receive a stable land inheritance. As it happened, Yakov's words came true. The tribe of Levi was given no land inheritance whatsoever. Concerning the tribe of Shimon, as Menachem Leibtag stated it: "Considering that Shimon's (land inheritance) is later included (almost 'swallowed up)

8 Yehudah, your brothers will give you praise. Your hand will be on the back of your enemies' necks; your father's sons will prostrate themselves before you.[5]

9 Yehudah is a lion cub. My son goes up to the hunt; he stalks, lying down like a lion. Like a young lion, who can flush him out?

10 The king's royal scepter will not be taken away from Yehudah, nor legal authority from his midst, until the Messiah comes, and nations will be gathered around him.[6]

11 His young donkey is strapped to a vine; his female donkey's colt to the best vine. His clothes are washed in wine, and his robes in grape juice.[7]

12 His eyes are maroon from wine, and his teeth white from milk.

13 Zevulun will live by the seashore, the area where ships frequent. The farmost part of his territory is by Sidon.[8]

14 Yissachar is a bony donkey that lies down between the animal pens.

15 He has seen that his place of rest is good, and that the Land is pleasing. So he will become a manual laborer and become a poorly paid servant.

16 Dan will judge his people when all the tribes of Israel are united as one.[9]

---

within the borders of Yehuda (see Yehoshua [the book of Joshua] 9.1 and 19.9), one could conclude that Shimon basically never received their own (land inheritance, a fulfillment of Yaakov's 'blessing' to Shimon in Breishit [Bereshit] 48.5–7)." "Shiurim in Chumash & Navi," The Tanach Study Center," n.d. http://www.tanach.org/dvarim/vzot.txt (accessed September 7, 2009).

5. *v.* 8: This verse is full of word plays, leading me to believe that it was meant to be memorized, with its word plays making it easier to do so. We have "Yehudah" (the proper name), followed by *yoduka* ("will praise you") and then *yadeka* ("your hand").

6. *v.10:* I have translated the name "Shiloh" as "Messiah", following the Targum, and much of Jewish Torah interpretation.

7. *v.11:* The Targum translates this verse entirely different, with *ayyar* (young donkey) translated alternatively as the word *ir'*(city). This is an interesting rendition that I do not dismiss. Yet I translate v. 11 as a poetic couplet; that is, both parts of the sentence are describing the same young donkey.

8. *v.13:* Sidon is a port city in today's Lebanon.

9. *v.16:* An alternative rendering may be "Dan will judge his people as if the tribes of Israel were united as one." Both translations belie simple explanation. I do not know of a time period in history when the tribe of Dan, or its judges, were famous as legal authorities throughout Israel. Can it be possible that Yakov was referring to Samson, one of Dan's

17 Dan will be a snake on the road, a viper on the path that bites a horse's heel. Its rider will fall backwards![10]

18 I have hoped for your deliverance, O God!

19 Gad will be assaulted by a band of attackers, but he will have success in pursuing them.

20 Asher will provide rich food, doling out delicacies fit for a king.

21 Naftali is a doe that has been freed, who teaches wonderful things.

22 Joseph is fruitful, and flourishes like a vine that grows by water springs; like a vine that creeps up a high wall.

23 Archers will make his life bitter by hating him and fighting against him.[11]

24 Yet his bow will be firm, and his arms will prevail because of the Warrior of Yakov, the Shepherd, the Rock of Israel!

---

descendants, who judged Israel? (cf. Judges 13—16)? Interestingly, the Targum interprets vv.16–18 to be speaking of a Messianic figure, with its words, "From the house of Dan will be chosen and will arise a man in whose days his people will be redeemed, and in whose years the tribes of Israel will rest altogether. The man who shall be chosen shall arise from the house of Dan; his terror shall be thrown on the nations, and his smiting will be strengthened among the Philistines; like a venomous serpent lying on the road, and like a viper that lies in wait on the path, he will slaughter the giants of the camps of the Philistines, horsemen with foot soldiers; He will hamstring the horses and chariots, and will overthrow their riders backwards. For your deliverance I wait, O Lord" (Clem translation). Tractate Pesachim 5b of the Talmud preserves an interesting awareness of these words of Yakov about the tribe of Dan. It is written: "There was a man who used to go about and at every opportunity would say "Dono Dini" (Judge ye my judgment). Whence it was inferred that the man was one of the tribe of Dan, concerning whom it is written [Gen. xlix. 16]: "Dan shall judge his people, as one of the tribes of Israel." Tractate Pasachem, Chapter 1: "Regulations concerning the removal of leaven from the house on the eve of Passover and the exact time when this must be accomplished," *Jewish Virtual Library*. n.d. http://www.jewishvirtuallibrary.org/jsource/Talmud/pesach1.html (accessed September 7, 2009). Although the exact intent of the utterances of this tribe of Dan member is not clear, there was awareness among the *Amoraim* (the rabbis quoted in the Gemara) of this predicted role for that tribe. It explained his abnormal behavior. This awareness was based on Yakov's words in Bereshit 49.16, which are quoted in the Talmudic text.

10. *vv.17 and 19*: Both use the Hebrew word *akev* in the text, which would draw the attention of the ancient hearer or reader. In v. 17 it describes the horse's "heel"; in *v.* 19, I translated the word as pursuing after them, literally being, "at the heels."

11. *v. 23*: The Hebrew word *aleh* is used in both verses 22 and 23. Again, this is a poetic play on words causing a rhyme in the Hebrew poetry. That is, "Joseph is a *vine* (*aleh*, *v.* 22); and "archers (*b'aleh chitzim*) shot at him" (*v.* 23).

25 The God of your fathers, and your Helper is the Almighty. He will bless you with blessings from Heaven, and blessings upon earth, then blessings of the breast and womb.

26 The blessings from *your* father will be beyond the blessings of *my* parents, rising all the way up to the desired eternal hills. This will be for Joseph's head, and for the top of the heads of his chosen brothers.[12]

27 Binyamin is a predatory wolf. In the morning he captures his prey and eats it until the evening, when he divides up his capture."

28 These make up the twelve tribes of Israel, and this is what their father said to them as he blessed them. He blessed each one with his own specific blessing.

29 He instructed them and said to them: "I will be gathered to my people; bury me with my fathers in the cave that is in the field of Efron the Hittite,

30 in the cave that is in the field at Macpelah which is beside Mamre in the land of Canaan. Avraham bought this field from Efron the Hittite for a burial plot.

31 It's there that Avraham and his wife Sarah are buried, and Isaac and his wife Rivka are buried; and it's there that I buried Leah.

32 The field as well as the cave that's in it were bought from the sons of Chet."

33 Yakov finished giving instructions to his sons, and then he curled up on his bed and breathed his last breath. So he died.[13]

12. *v.* 26: This verse is written in poetic and cryptic language. Many versions differ in their translations of this verse; e.g., the JPS translation states: "The blessings of your father surpass the blessings of my ancestors, to the utmost bounds of the eternal hills." The Targum reads: "The blessings of your father will be added to the blessings that my fathers blessed me, which the leaders that are from the world longed for. All these shall be on the head of Joseph, the most famous man of his brothers." Because of the difficult task of accurately translating some of these poetic idioms, the reader will find 49.26 translated in various manners. Perhaps here there is a likening of the height (a symbol of greatness) of Joseph and his brothers to the height of the hills of Judea and Samaria (termed the "mountains of Israel" in the book of Ezekiel).

13. *v.* 33: The Torah idiom "gathered to his people" (*lehe'asef el-ha'am*), which I translated as "then he died", refers to the end result of the death and burial process. The idiom literally means to be buried where one's ancestors are buried. In Yakov's case, this refers to burial at the Macpelah cave in the Land of Israel (cf. *vv.* 29–32).

Chapter 50

1   Joseph then fell upon his father's body, hugging and kissing it.

2   Joseph ordered the physicians who served him to embalm his father. So the doctors embalmed Israel.

3   The process of embalming him took forty days, as is usual for embalming. Egypt mourned seventy days for him.

4   After the days of mourning passed, Joseph spoke with Pharaoh's royal court, saying,

5   "Would you please do me a favor? Speak with Pharaoh, and tell him that I swore an oath to my father. He told me, 'I am dying and want to be buried in the tomb that I dug over in the land of Canaan.' Now, I request permission to go up there and bury my father, after which I will return."

6   Pharaoh replied, "Go ahead, go and bury your father as you swore to him that you would."

7   So Joseph went up to bury his father. All of Pharaoh's servants traveled with him, including the elders of his court and those of the land of Egypt.

8   In addition, all of Joseph's family and his brothers, as well as his father's household, went up.

9   Chariots and mounted cavalry also went up. This caravan was a very large one.

10 They all arrived at the threshing floor of Atad, on the far side of the Jordan, and for one week they mourned greatly for his father.

11 The inhabitants of the land of Canaan saw the mourning at the threshing floor of Atad. They said to each other, "These Egyptians are mourning deeply." And so they called this very place, which is on the far side of the Jordan, "The Egyptian mourning place."

12 His (Israel's) sons did exactly what he instructed them to do.

13 His sons brought his body to the land of Canaan, and they buried him in the cave at the field of Machpelah. Avraham bought this field for a burial site from Efron the Hittite, (who was) from the region of Mamre.

14 After burying his father, Joseph returned to Egypt; he and his brothers and everyone who went with them to bury his father.

15 Then Joseph's brothers lived in great fear because their father had died. They said amongst themselves, "What if Joseph is bitter towards us, and pays us back for all the evil that we did to him?"

16 They then instructed Joseph, saying, "Your father gave us an order before he died. He said:

17 'Tell the following to Joseph: Please forgive the crimes and evil acts that your brothers committed against you. Forgive the crimes of the servants of your father's God.'" Joseph wept when they spoke these very words to him.

18 His brothers approached him and bowed down before him. They said, "Here, take us as your slaves."

19 But Joseph told them, "Don't be afraid. Am I second in command to God?

20 What you planned for evil toward me, God turned into good, so that this day would come, and many lives would be spared.

21 Now, don't be afraid of me! I will provide for all your needs; and for your children, too." He comforted them, and spoke compassionately to them.

22 So Joseph and his father's clan lived in Egypt. Joseph lived to be 110 years old.

23 Joseph lived to see his great-grandchildren through Ephraim, as well as his great-grandchildren through Makir, who was Menashe's son. (These great-grandchildren through Makir) were born on Joseph's knees.

24 Then Joseph said to his brothers, "I am dying. God will certainly visit you by taking you out of this land to the Land that was sworn to Avraham, Isaac and Yakov."

25 Joseph had his brothers take an oath, stating that, "When God visits you, you will bring my bones out of here, with you."[1]

26 So Joseph died at 110 years old, and he was embalmed and put into a coffin in Egypt.[2]

---

1. *v.* 25: This oath was fulfilled, according to the written texts of Exodus 13.19 and of Joshua 24.32: "So Moses took the bones of Joseph with him, because the sons of Israel swore an oath, declaring, 'God will really visit you, and you will bring up my bones from here with you' (Exodus 13.19, author's translation). "The bones of Joseph, that the sons of Israel had taken up out of Egypt, were buried in Shechem, in the part of the field that Yakov had bought from the sons of Hamor, the father of Shechem, for 100 kasitas. They constituted part of the land inheritance of the sons of Joseph" (Joshua 24.32, author's translation). It would make a fascinating linguistic and historical study to see what is being referred to by the word "they" in v. 25 (i.e., the land itself, or the bones). The burial tomb of Joseph has been identified as being in Nablus (modern day Shechem). From 1967–2000, Israelis visited this site and prayed there. Because the second intifada starting in 2000 resulted in unrest and terrorism, Israelis have not been allowed to visit the site regularly.

2. *v.*26: For funerary practices in ancient Egypt, see "Burial customs from late Middle Kingdom to Second Intermediate Period (about 1850–1550 BC)," Digital Egypt for Universities, 2001, http://www.digitalegypt.ucl.ac.uk/burialcustoms/latemk.html (accessed September 7, 2009). This period best coincides with Joseph's lifetime.

Glossary

Akeida: Hebrew for "binding," referring to the binding of Isaac by Avraham. In Jewish thought, it is an awe-inspiring passage, thus I give it some introductory attention.

Amoraim: The rabbis/teachers who are quoted in the Gemara portion of the Talmud.

Avot: The biblical patriarchs Avraham, Isaac, Yakov, and Yakov's sons.

Avram: More commonly known as Abram.

Avraham: More commonly known as Abraham.

Bereshit: Literally, in Hebrew, "in the beginning." This is also the name for the book of Genesis.

Bet-El: More commonly known as Bethel.

Bereshit Rabbah: One book in a series of midrashic commentaries to the Written Torah. It features stories that embellish the text of Bereshit. Some assign its origin to the third century, in the Land of Israel. I refer the reader to the short article on Bereshit Rabbah found at: http://www.jewish encyclopedia.com/view.jsp?artid=822&letter=B.

Binyamin: More commonly known as Benjamin.

Chava: More commonly known as Eve.

Chutzpah: Hebrew for "intestinal fortitude," "guts," or more generally, bravery. Sometimes in colloquial Hebrew and Yiddish it carries a negative connotation, i.e., an overly pushy or aggressive person.

Epic of Gilgamesh: Ancient Sumerian text, found on twelve clay tablets, that recounts the adventure of the hero Gilgamesh as he seeks immortality.

Esav: More commonly known as Esau.

First Enoch: A pseudepigraphic work of Jewish religious literature, attributed to an anonymous first century BC author. The work explains the heavenly visions of the biblical figure Hanoch (Enoch). "Pseudepigraphic" refers to the work being non-canonical but attributed to be works of biblical figures (like Hanoch). About twenty-seven different ancient works are thought of as pieces of pseudepigraphic literature.

Halakah: A Hebrew term in religious literature and Jewish jurisprudence that means "according to extant legal ruling," or interpretation. As well, it can mean doing something according to given custom. As a general term it can refer to the Jewish people's way of life in a given time period and location.

HaShem: Literally, "the Great Name" or "the Great Reputation," i.e. God.

Hevel: More commonly known as Abel.

Ibn Ezra: Avraham Ibn Ezra, the famous Jewish rabbi and Torah commentator from Andalusia, d. 1167.

Kayin: More commonly known as Cain.

Land: The Land of Israel. I capitalize it as a sign of respect for the holiness of the physical land.

Mekilta d'Rabbi Yishma'el: A midrashic work on certain chapters of the book of Exodus, attributed to the authorship of Rabbi Yishma'el, a Tannaitic sage.

Midrash: A style of Jewish biblical interpretation that embellishes the text with stories that are external to the text in order to bring out or illustrate important moral lessons. These stories also investigate possibilities of meaning for a particular portion of scripture.

Mishnah: The earlier portion of the Talmud, codified in approximately the year 200 by Rabbi Yehudah.

Mitzvah: One of God's instructions or teachings, either found in the scriptures or defined as such by accepted Jewish custom. In idiomatic Hebrew, it is an act of compassion that is done for someone else's benefit.

Mitzvot: Plural of mitzvah. These are God's instructions or teachings, and can mean the 613 commandments or the full body of the scriptures. In idiomatic Hebrew, it means acts of compassion or goodness that are in fulfillment of what the scriptures instruct us to do.

Ramban: The acronym of Rabbi Moshe ben Nachman, d. 1270, another one of Judaism's foremost scholars and commentators.

Rashi: The acronym of Rabbi Shlomo Yitzhaki, d. 1105, one of Judaism's foremost Biblical and Talmudic commentators.

Rivkah: More commonly known as Rebecca.

Talmud: The Mishna and the Gemara. This is a rabbinic compendium of Jewish life originating from discussions and deliberations in the yeshivas of Israel, and later Babylon (the Persian Empire) from approximately 150 BC to 550 AD.

Tanna: A rabbi quoted in the Mishnah, whose lifetime was anytime between 10 AD to 220 AD.

Targum: The Aramaic translation and interpretation of the Hebrew text of the Bible. The most popular Targum is named "Targum Onkelos," and is a late first century or early 2nd century work of a Jewish translator named Onkelos. The Targum gives many relevant and important insights into how the first century Babylonian Jewish community understood the Torah. This community comprised approximately twenty-five percent of the worldwide Jewish community of that era, if not more.

Targum Neofiti: A version of the Targum covering Genesis-Deuteronomy.

Targum Yonatan: A version of the Targum attributed to be the work of Yonatan ben Uzziel, a chief student of Hillel. This work translates the Prophets.

Torah: This word has three possible meanings: the five books of Moses; all of the written scriptures (Genesis-Malachi); or both of the previous meanings plus a great body of rabbinic Jewish religious literature, which definition would include the Talmud. The context determines which definition is valid for its given use.

Yakov: More commonly known as Jacob.

Bibliography

Alexander, Philip S. *Textual Sources for the Study of Judaism*. Chicago, IL: University of Chicago Press, 1990.

Bernstein, Amy. "Endless Enigmas." *Mysteries of Science, Special Edition of U.S. News and World Report* (2009) 4–7.

The Bible: The New International Version. Grand Rapids, MI: Zondervan Publishing, 2003.

Clem, Eldon, trans. "*Targum Jonatan Isaiah*." Unpublished document.

———, trans. "*Translation of Targum Onkelos and Jonathan*." Tulsa, OK: Oaktree Software, 2006. CD-ROM.

Epstein, Dr. I., ed. *Soncino Babylonian Talmud*. London, England: The Soncino Press, 1948.

Friedman, David. *Who Knows Abba Arika*. Hampton, VA: Shoreshim Publishers, 2005.

Hawking, Stephen. *A Brief History of Time*. New York, NY: Bantam Books, 1990.

JPS Tanakh/The Jewish Bible. Philadelphia, PA: The Jewish Publication Society, 2007.

Kass, Leon. *The Beginning of Wisdom*. New York, NY: Simon & Schuster, 2003.

Keleman, Rabbi Lawrence. *Permission to Believe*. Southfield, MI: Targum Press, 1990.

Patai, Raphael. *The Messiah Texts*. Detroit, MI: Wayne State University Press, 1989.

Riskin, Shlomo. "There is still time". *Jerusalem Post*, October 24, 2008, final edition, p. 42.

Scherman, Nosson, and Meir Zlotowitz, eds. *Tashlich*. Brooklyn, NY: Mesorah Publications, 2006.

Schonfeld, Z. E. *To Fathom Darkness 1940–1945*. Jerusalem, Israel: privately printed, 1983.

Schroeder, Gerald. *Genesis and the Big Bang Theory*. New York, NY: Bantam Books, 1991.

Shem, H. J. *A Proto-Semitic Grammar and Textbook*. No location given: Winged Bull Press, 2006.

Singer, Binyamin. *Ramban. Volume 1*. Southfield, MI: Targum Press, 2000.

Soloveitchik, Rabbi J. *The Lonely Man of Faith*. New York, NY: Doubleday Publishing, 2006.

Steinsaltz, Rabbi Adin. *Biblical Images*. New York, NY: Basic Books, 1984.

Stern, David, trans. *The Complete Jewish Bible*. Clarksville, MD: Jewish New Testament Publications, 1998.

Wade, Nicholas. "Adam, Eve and the Genome." *Mysteries of Science, Special Edition of U.S. News and World Report* (2009) 42–47.

Westbrook, Raymond. "Good as His Word." *Biblical Archaeology Review* (May/June 2009) 50–55, 64.

Internet Resources

Disclaimer: The author assumes no responsibility for website address changes at the time of this book's publication.

Algavish, David. "Daf Parashat HaShavua: Parshat Vayishlakh." www.biu.ac.il/JH/Parasha/eng/vayishlach/alga.html.

Amar, Zohar. "Daf Parashat HaShavua: Parshat Vayishlakh." http://www.biu.ac.il/JH/Parasha/eng/vayishlach/vayish1.html.

Bar-da, Amos. "Making the Crooked Straight." http://www.biu.ac.il/JH/Parasha/eng/vayetze/ amo.html.

Barkai, Gavriel. "The Exodus." Lecture, Bet Israel Synagogue, Jerusalem, Israel, April 6, 2003.

"Book of Enoch." http://reluctantmessenger.com/book_of_enoch.htm.

Burstein, Marcus. "Jacob Adopts Ephraim and Manasseh." http://www.jewishaz.com/jewishnews/041224/torah.shtml.

Charles, R. H., trans. "Book of Enoch." http://www.sacred-texts.com/bib/boe/.

Elgavish, David. "Jacob's Treaty with Laban." http://www.biu.ac.il/JH/Parasha/eng/vayetze/ elga.html.

Fields, Weston. "Salted With Fire." http:/www.jerusalemperspective.com/Default.aspx tabid=27&ArticleID=145.

Frand, Yissocher. "Rabbi Frand on Parshas Vayishlach." http://www.torah.org/learning/ravfrand/5757/vayishlach.html?print=1.

The Gnostic Society Library. "The Coming of Melkizedek." http://www.gnosis.org/library/commelc.htm.

Goldberg, Hillel. "Does order in the Torah make a difference?" http://www.jewishworldreview.com/hillel/goldberg_2003_11_28.

"Happy New Year: The Times and the Seasons." http://unitedisrael.org/blog/2009/03/26/happy-new-year-the-times-and-the-seasons/.

Hattin, Michael. "The Legacy of Kayin." http://vbm-torah.org/archive/intparsha66/01-66bereishit.htm.

Huehnergard, John. "Proto-Semitic Language and Culture." http://www.bartleby.com/61/10. html.

Institute for Creation Research. http://www.icr.org/bible/gen/.

Jakobovici, Simcha, producer. *The Exodus* (documentary film). The History Channel, 4/22/09. (History.com).

Kaveh, Moshe. "The Beginning of the Universe, the Beginning of Life and the Beginning of Wisdom." http://www.biu.ac.il/JH/Parasha/eng/bereshit/kaveh.html.

Landau, Dov. "But to Cain and his offering He paid no heed." http://www.biu.ac.il/JH/Parasha/eng/bereshit/lan.html.

Leibtag, Menachem. "Parashat Ve-Zot Ha-Bracha." http://www.tanach.org/dvarim/vzot.txt.

Levin, Y. "The Meaning of TMM in Gen. 25:27," e-mail to b-hebrew mailing list, July 12, 2007, http://lists.ibiblio.org/ pipermail/b-hebrew/2007-July/032880.html.

Levy, Eric. "The Sin of the B'nei Ha'Elohim." http://www.ericlevy.com/Writings/Writings_BneiElohim.htm.

Lichtmann, Moshe. "Do Not Bury Me in Egypt." http://www.torahmitzion.org/pub/parsha/5768/ vayechi.pdf.

Madigan, Brian. "Ancient Egyptian Bread Making." http://www.mnsu.edu/emuseum/prehistory/ egypt/dailylife/breadmaking.htm.

ORT organization, "Navigating the Bible II: VaYishlach." http://bible.ort.org/books/Torahd5.asp?action=displayid&id=1065, "VaYishlach."

Philologos. "Back to Mamre." http://www.forward.com/articles/12049.

Pinner, Daniel. "Vayeshev: In exile, redemption." http://www.israelnationalnews.com/Articles/ Article.aspx/8448.

Prince, John D., Wilhelm Bacher, and M. Seligsohn. "Teraphim." www.jewishencyclopedia
.com /view.jsp? artid=150&letter=T.

Resnick, Liebel. "Egyptology and Torah. http://www.aish.com/societyWork/sciencenature/
Egyptology_in_the_Torah_Biblical_Archeology.asp.

Riskin, Shlomo. "Parashat Vayetze: In goats' clothing." http://fr.jpost.com/servlet/Satellite
?cid=1227702430721&pagename=JPArticle%2FShowFull.

———. "The Leaders and the Led." http://pqasb.pqarchiver.com/jpost/access/1622248341
.html?dids=1622248341:1622248341&FMT=ABS&FM.

Sarfatti, Gad. "Did the Patriarchs Speak Hebrew?" http://www.biu.ac.il/JH/Parasha/eng/
vayigash/vayigash.shtml.

Seawright, Caroline. "Ancient Egyptian Alcohol." http://www.thekeep.org/~kunoichi/
kunoichi/ themestream/egyptalcohol.html.

"Shiurim in Chumash and Navi." http://www.tanach.org/dvarim/vzot.txt.

Sobolofsky, Zvi. "Yakov and Israel, A Dual Destiny." http://www.torahweb.org/torah/1999/
parsha/rsob_vayishlach.html.

Spiegel, Ya'akov. "Rachel's Tombstone: The Reasons for Erecting a Tombstone." http://
www.biu.ac.il/JH/Parasha/eng/vayishlach/vayish1.html.

Steinhardt, David. "Parshat Noah 5768." http://www.bnaitorah.org/clientuploads/
sermons/Rabbi_Steinhardt_Parsha_Noah_5768_2.pdf).

"Teraphim." http://www.jewishencyclopedia.com/view.jsp?artid=150&letter=T

"Tractate Berakhot." http://www.e-daf.com/index.asp.

"Tractate Eruvin." http://www.e-daf.com/index.asp.

"Tractate Pesachim." http://www.jewishvirtuallibrary.org/jsource/Talmud/pesach1.html.

"Tractate Rosh Hashanah." http://www.jewishvirtuallibrary.org/jsource/Talmud/rh1
html

"Tractate Shabbat." http://www.jewishvirtuallibrary.org/jsource/Talmud/ shabbat12.
html.

"Tractate Ta'anit." http://www.jewishvirtuallibrary.org/jsource/Talmud/taanit1.html.

"Tractate Ta'anit." http://www.e-daf.com/index.asp.

University College, London, England, editors. "Burial customs from late Middle Kingdom
to Second Intermediate Period (about 1850–1550 BC)." http://www.digitalegypt.ucl.
ac.uk/burialcustoms/latemk.html.